How to find your soul m
wholeness that

Soul Mate
Or
Just Another Date

"And the LORD God said, It is not good that the man should be alone; I will make him an help meet for him." Genesis 2:18

Dexter L. Jones & Prophetess Brenda Boykin

Wasteland Press
Shelbyville, KY USA
www.wastelandpress.net

Soul Mate or Just Another Date
by Dexter L. Jones & Prophetess Brenda Boykin

Copyright © 2008 Dexter L. Jones and Prophetess Brenda Boykin
ALL RIGHTS RESERVED
ISBN: 978-1-60047-231-2
First Printing—August 2008

NO PART OF THIS BOOK MAY BE REPRODUCED IN ANY FORM, BY PHOTOCOPYING OR BY ANY ELECTRONIC OR MECHANICAL MEANS, INCLUDING INFORMATION STORAGE OR RETRIEVAL SYSTEMS, WITHOUT PERMISSION IN WRITING FROM THE COPYRIGHT OWNERS/AUTHORS

Unless otherwise indicated, Scripture quotations in this book are from the King James Version of the Bible.

This publication is designed to provide information in regard to the subject matter covered. It is published with the understanding that the authors are not engaged in rendering legal counsel or other professional services. If legal advice or other professional advice is required, the services of a professional person should be sought.

Printed in the U.S.A.

Dedication – Dexter L. Jones

I dedicate this book to my Heavenly Father God, my Lord and Savior Jesus Christ and the Person of the Holy Spirit. *"For there are three that bear record in heaven, the Father, the Word, and the Holy Ghost: and these three are one." 1 John 5:7*

As always I dedicate this book also to my precious daughter Jasmine Shonte' Jones, a daughter that I am so proud of and that I love so dearly. Jasmine, the three most important things in life are your relationship with God, finding your purpose in life, and allowing God to bring you together with your soul mate. I am so confident that God shall establish all three for you, so that you can go forth whole and complete in every area of your life, *Daddy.* I also dedicate this book to the greatest mother in the world, my mother, Edna M. Artis. I love you very much.

Dedication – Prophetess Brenda Boykin

I dedicate this book to my wonderful husband Pastor James Boykin and our precious children, Nekeisha, Victor, Joiquan and Andrianna, and to my wonderful grandchildren, Kayla and CJ. I say thank you for loving me for who I am. To the women, I take my strength, courage and beautiful looks. Mommy, (Lorranine Thompson) thank you for instilling great values in me; you have always been there for me. Your love for me is endless. I watch you over the years work hard and your hard work has paid off. Also, to my dear heart, Tijuana and my two big brother, James and Frankie, thank you for being my earthly protectors. To my aunt, the twenty-five cents you gave to me to buy candy, I spent it after church. Thanks for never judging me and making me feel I could do anything. To my wonderful church Family Deliverance Powerhouse Praise Ministry. I also want to say, love you to my three best friends, Delores Eppes, Cynthia Pippens and James King, thank you for all the years of unselfish love.

Also, special thanks to Ayanna Pippen for taking the time to edit this book, we couldn't have done it without you. A millions thanks for your time and your efforts, we love you.

Contents

Introduction		1
Chapter 1	Adam and Eve	3
Chapter 2	Broken Relationships and Broken Promises	10
Chapter 3	Finding a Good Thing	15
Chapter 4	Soul Mate Course	20
Chapter 5	Friend to Friend	34
Chapter 6	Are You Attracting Your Soul Mate	38
Chapter 7	Your Ideal Soul Mate	48
Chapter 8	Attracting Your Soul Mate A. Deep calleth unto the Deep	59 62
Chapter 9	God's Divine Plan for Your Life	73
Chapter 10	Meditation Guarantees You Success	75
Chapter 11	God's Ideal Relationship	81
Chapter 12	The Ten Elements of Truth	91
Chapter 13	Ten Ways to Know If You've Met Your Soul Mate	93
Chapter 14	Ten Questions to Ask to See If You've Met Your Soul Mate	97
Chapter 15	Twelve Authoritative Prayers to Bind And Blast Away Just Another Date	102

Chapter 16	Twelve Authoritative Prayers to Loose And Attract Your Ideal Soul Mate	104
Chapter 17	Walk in Love	106

A Word From the Heart of Dexter L. Jones

I am deeply touched with the heart cry of individuals that truly desire to live before God and who have the gift of marriage, but have not had the privilege of experiencing the fulfillment of that gift with their true soul mate.

Life is short. Even if we're blessed to live one hundred years on the earth, this is still only a brief span when we realize the wonder and beauty of life and the greatness of the God we serve.

Daily, individuals are becoming more and more frustrated because they have not yet found their true soul mate. My heart yearns for you because I desire to see you complete in all areas of your life.

I want you to be happy in your relationship and finally in marriage. I desire to see your soul mate and you rejoicing over the goodness of God, in what he has done in bringing you together as you rejoice over each other.

This book was written to magnify and glorify the Father because Jesus understands what you're going through and the temptations you face. I know there are multitudes that are crying daily to God for answers and direction, well this book is for you. Because others are seeking also, it's up to you to pass the word along to others that are single and desire to find their soul mate, as you bless others, God will also bless you.

God is for you not against you. He wants you to be happy complete and fulfilled in every area of your life. He made you and he understands your spiritual, mental and sexual needs.

Go forth with faith and hope and *"knowing that all things work together for good to them that love God, to them who are the called according to his purpose." Romans 8:28*

The soul mate that you're desiring is also desiring you, the yearning in them is calling the yearning in you, the deep in you is calling the deep in them and the longing in you is calling for the longing in them.

You can do it. You can find your soul mate in the 21st century and experience the wholeness that God has designed for your life.

A Word From The Heart of Prophetess Brenda Boykin

My prayer goes out to all of those who are awaiting a godly soul mate. As women we must understand that we were not made to be hunters. We should never position ourselves to seek for a mate. As Daddy's Little Girls we don't look for a mate; put all your effort in chasing after the Father. A true fact is that men are attractive to women that don't appear to be needy. If you and I are seeking first the kingdom of God, then as women after His own heart, the bible promise that God will supply all our needs. Godly men who are searching for their mate want women who are spiritual and emotionally stable. The only way we can be completely whole is for us as women to be found in the secret place of the most High. Believe me, men are equipped to hunt, God has equipped them for such a task. Men who truly love God don't mind going into the secret place to find their mate. If they find you there, their heart will always trust in you as long as you stay in the secret place.

It is in that secret place that you learn, not to gamble with your heart. It is there your heart belongs to God.

Your soul mate is looking for you, be prepared when he or she comes. Don't be like the five brides; they were not ready when the bride groom came. You will know that they are your soul mate, because at that moment you will have a release and desire to fulfill your destiny together that God's has so wonderfully ordain for you both. The key is to be ready for both of you to move together.

You hear people say all the time, it seem like I have known you for a long time. It is because, you are really that person's other half that they have been missing. Even though you may have just met, you have been communicating with each other in the spirit and that is what happen when destiny meet time.

God bless you with your soul mate.

Introduction

Within these pages are the answers that you've been seeking. Answers concerning questions that has arisen in your mind and prayers that you have petitioned God about concerning your soul mate.

Many men and women have been through many broken relationships and broken promises only to come to the conclusion that the individual they thought was their soul mate turned out to be just another date.

Some of the dates have been brief and some have extended to months and years with much wasted time, effort and money. Many have become frustrated as a result and some have even abandoned the idea of ever finding their true soul mate.

Others have come to the conclusion that maybe there is no such thing as a soul mate and decided to settle for less than the best for their life.

Individuals have made finding their soul mate more of a job and task than the enjoyment that God has designed for this to be. We have made finding our soul mate a rigorous and painstaking effort, when it's really so easy to do.

Many individuals are unaware of the signals they're sending out and they're repelling their soul mate instead of attracting them. Well in this book, we will teach you how to stop repelling your soul mate and begin to do the things necessary to attract your soul mate.

The very things that you will learn we have used ourselves and it has worked for us and many others that have desired to find their soul mate.

When you begin to apply these truths to your life, the negativity and hindrances that have attached itself to you will begin to unravel and unstitch itself and the positive and spiritual will begin to work for you.

"And all things, whatsoever ye shall ask in prayer, believing, ye shall receive. And nothing shall be impossible unto you." Matthew 21:22, 17:20

1

Adam and Eve

"And the LORD God caused a deep sleep to fall upon Adam, and he slept: and he took one of his ribs, and closed up the flesh instead thereof; And the rib, which the LORD God had taken from man, made he a woman, and brought her unto the man. And Adam said, This is now bone of my bones, and flesh of my flesh: she shall be called Woman, because she was taken out of Man." Genesis 2:21-23

Before God made Adam he brought forth many different creatures and these creatures had an opposite, a male and female "but for Adam there was *not found a help meet for him." Genesis 2:20b*

"And the LORD God said, It is not good that the man should be alone; I will make him an help meet for him." Genesis 2:18 So God made a help meet for the man. *"And Adam called his wife's name Eve; because she was the mother of all living." Genesis 3:20*

When God made a help meet for Adam it was because he did not want Adam to be alone he wanted Adam to have someone that he could worship God with, someone to fellowship with and someone to *"Be fruitful, and multiply, and replenish the earth and subdue it: and have dominion over the fish of the sea, and over the fowl of the air, and over every living thing that moveth upon the earth." Genesis 1:28*

God also wanted Adam to have someone to enjoy the beauty and splendor of the garden with, someone whom Adam could simply enjoy God's creation with and in return enjoy each other.

Adam and Eve were not just out on a date, but they were true soul mates and the word of God said, *"They shall be one flesh." Genesis 2:24b.* This oneness that God was promulgating (*emphasizing*) was that Adam and Eve shall be on one accord in spirit and soul. This is what it means to have a soul mate. Not every one is designed to be your soul mate.

God saw this oneness of Adam and Eve in such union and harmony that he saw them as one not two, one in unification and two in uniqueness. *"Male and female (uniqueness) created he them; and blessed them,* **and called their name Adam** *(unification), in the day when they were created." Genesis 5:2*

When God saw Adam and Eve in their uniqueness he saw in them their own individual personalities and characteristics, he did not see them as one in exactness or in robotic form. He was not trying to make them a clone or a carbon copy of each other.

God wanted Adam and Eve to keep their uniqueness, but have unification of spirit and soul.

Unification of spirit means to be *"equally yoked"* with one another first of all a believer with a believer, a believer must not be with an unbeliever. *"Be ye not unequally yoked together with unbelievers: for what fellowship hath righteousness with unrighteousness? And what communion hath light with darkness? And what concord hath Christ with Belial? Or what part hath he that believeth with an infidel? And what agreement hath the temple of God with idols?" 2 Corinthians 6:14-16a*

There is no such thing in God's book that says *if I date him or her I can be a good influence and they might get saved.* **No, (*here you're tempting the Lord*) follow the scriptures and you will be blessed.** Yet, unification of spirit is still not enough to qualify you as soul mates. This is one error that many are making, believing that because they're both believers, this will make them a perfect candidate for one another. This is a misconception and a fallacy to the highest degree.

Unification of spirit can also mean *"the same faith or beliefs."* Such a union will minimize the confusion and chaos that may try to enter in. If one of you are Catholic and the other is Pentecostal this could create problems and not because one is right and the other is wrong. There are true Jesus loving, God worshiping believers in both that follow only the scriptures.

The problem may arise in choosing which belief you will follow and what faith the children be raised in. It is true that people read the same Bible yet believe differently and here we're not talking major doctrine difference such as one believes that Jesus is not the Son of God and another believes that he is.

This is a major doctrinal error and these two individuals should never be joined together. Yet, if you're both Pentecostal, Catholic, Baptist etc. this will make for greater unity. If the beliefs of two different denominations are not far apart this could still work if the basic foundation of Christianity is present.

Unification of soul deals with a union of your intellects, wills, likes and emotions. Unification of souls also deals with compatibility, which is a major concern for a successful relationship and marriage. **I believe that this issue of**

compatibility is one of the major reasons for failure in relationships. I personally don't believe in the principle that opposites attract. This may work perfectly with scientific and electrical things, but with personalities and characteristics you're asking for trouble.

Unification of soul in the area of compatibility deserves to be taught about here in some length because a major problem arises when there is incompatibility.

1. *Incompatibility tells us to halt yet we do not listen.*

2. *Incompatibility tells us this is inappropriate yet we go on with full speed ahead.*

3. *Incompatibility tells us this is unsuitable yet we plunge forward with great velocity.*

4. *Incompatibility tells us there is incongruity (imbalance) here yet with swiftness we pursue our endeavor.*

These discrepancies and differences in compatibility cause us to do opposite of what the other would do and provoke much frustration and chaos in the relationship.

When God created Adam he gave him a help meet that was compatible with him in unification of soul, he didn't give him someone that would cause frustration and confusion within the relationship and marriage.

We're not talking perfection here by any means, but we're talking unity and oneness of souls, concurring, agreeing and understanding. This does not mean that you will agree and concur on everything, but it does mean that the two of you have an understanding and you can disagree without being disagreeable. You're both on the same sheet of music playing the same tune in spite of your individual and unique personalities.

When God caused a deep sleep to fall upon Adam he took out of Adam a piece of him and made an help meet that was unified with him in spirit and soul. This help meet was closely aligned with him because she came from him.

Many individuals are not God's best choice for you. If God had to find help meets as he did for Adam by taking a rib **the majority of individuals we're with today are not the ones God would have taken out**.

Most individuals today whether in dating or marriage are not with their soul mates, but just another date. (*Let's get something very clear here, we're not promoting divorce, we're just stating a truth and fact. The divorce rate confirms this fact.*)

When people ask those individuals that are truly happy in relationships and marriage how did they know this individual was for them, most will respond by saying ***"you just know."***
However, we think this response is too general and vague. It has no real substance to base an understanding on; the statement while sincere is unclear. The thought expressed is true and the most appropriate answer the individual can give at that time and their best explanation.

Yet the enquirer walks away still unclear about how they will know and what to look for. We know that a majority of the answer is compatibility; not just on one or two things but many things along with a witness or peace in your spirit that tells you this is the one.

Therefore, as you establish a greater relationship with God and listen to the voice of the Holy Spirit and your own spirit along with the things you will learn in this book, you will be led of the spirit and find the true soul mate of your life.

Unification of soul also deals with a union of mental beliefs and principles concerning certain matters and situations that occur in life. Here we're not referring to petty or small things that will fall more in the line of your individual preferences, but more major things that could cause a rift in the relationship. *Example 1: Some Christians may believe that it's ok to have premarital sex while others believe in totally obeying the scriptures and abstaining from sex before marriage.*

Example 2: Some Christians may believe that you don't have to go to church every Sunday, once a month is fine for them while others believe that you should be in church every Sunday. Such a disharmony of souls could be disastrous and create confusion and chaos in the relationship.

When individuals are looking to find or be found of their soul mates they are mostly on a course destined for failure simply because they don't know how to look for their soul mates.

Males and females are following more of the world's way of thinking than the Bible's way of thinking. In the world the most important issue is physical attraction *(We agree there must be some physical attraction to the individual),* but physical attraction should not be priority one on your list.

The world's method of finding a mate is body or physical attraction first and next soul or mental attraction.

The word and God's method of finding a mate is first the spirit, second the soul and last the body. The scripture even accentuates the specific order of importance saying *"And the very God of peace sanctify you wholly; and I pray God your whole spirit and soul and body be preserved blameless unto the coming of our Lord Jesus Christ." 1 Thessalonians 5:23*

When God brought Eve to Adam they were unified in spirit first, unified in soul second and the body held such a low concern that *"they were both naked, the man and his wife, and were not ashamed." Genesis 2:25*

As a saint of God you must realize that when you are unified in spirit and soul that makes everything else beautiful, but when you're not unified the greatest physical attraction cannot produce the celebration of love that only comes when two are one in spirit and soul unification.

This is the only kind of true love that has staying and keeping power in a relationship and eventually in marriage. If you will notice that even though Adam and Eve disobeyed God and caused much trouble for mankind, according to the scriptures they still remain married and unified with each other. The scriptures records no divorce in the life of Adam and Eve even though they were married for over eight hundred years and the reason is because these two individual were not just on a date but were true soul mates. Genesis 5:4-5

2

Broken Relationships and Broken Promises

"A merry heart maketh a cheerful countenance: but by sorrow of the heart the spirit is broken. Sorrow is better than laughter: for by the sadness of the countenance the heart is made better." Proverbs 15:13, Ecclesiastes 7:3

Every person that has entered the world of dating has encountered or shall encounter a broken relationship and broken promises. No one is exempt from these two twins they run together like bosom buddies and cause much sorrow and sadness.

Yet, even these two twins can be turned into a positive if we're willing to learn from the experience they're teaching us. The scripture says *"but by sorrow of the heart the spirit is broken." Proverbs 15:13b*

There are positives that can be derived from a broken spirit if we will allow God to minister to us and heal the broken heart. The scripture says, *"He healeth the broken in heart, and bindeth up their wounds." Psalms 147:3*

No one is going to be exempt from broken relationships and broken promises but when it happens we can look to God to heal the broken heart and bind up that wound.

Individuals also miss what God is trying to show them because they fail to realize that God doesn't just want to heal the broken heart and bind up the wound, but he's trying to teach them something in the midst of it all.

God wants you to learn something and be the wiser the next time around, sad to say most individuals fail to get the message and encounter one broken heart after another.

There are individuals that have been married three, four, five, times or more before they learn the lessons of relationships, and others have had one relationship after another and always coming up with the short hand at the end of the relationship.

It's like the man in the scripture that refused to learn from the sorrow and heartaches derived from much drinking, so it goes: *"Who hath woe? who hath sorrow? Who hath contentions? Who hath babbling? Who hath wounds without cause? Who hath redness of eyes? They that tarry long at the wine; they that go to seek mixed wine. Look not upon the wine when it is red, when it giveth his colour in the cup, when it moveth itself aright. At the last it biteth like a serpent, and stingeth like an adder. Thine eyes shall behold strange women, and thine heart shall utter perverse things.*

Yea, thou shalt be as he that lieth down in the midst of the sea, or as he that lieth upon the top of a mast. **They have stricken me, shalt thou say, and I was not sick; they have beaten me, and I felt it not: when shall I awake? I will seek it yet again."** *Proverbs 23:29-35*

This individual even though he was beaten, has woe, sorrow, contentions, babbling, wounds without cause and redness of eyes, refuses to stop his drinking he continues to go at it over and over again blindly saying, *"I will seek it yet again."*

Well the individual that continues to make the same mistake in relationship and marriage and continues to choose the same type of individual is going to keep getting the same results.

The results of another broken relationship and a broken heart, wounds without cause, woe, contentions and sorrow of heart.

When will you awake?
When will you arise out of your sleep?
When will you open your eyes and ears?
When will you learn from your mistakes?
Why will you continue to be abused and misused?

A classic example of broken relationships and a broken heart is the story of The Samaritan Woman which can also be A Samaritan Man, so it goes; *"Jesus saith unto her, Go, call thy husband, and come hither. The woman answered and said, I have no husband. Jesus said unto her, Thou hast well said, I have no husband:* **For thou hast had five husbands; and he whom thou now hast is not thy husband:** *in that saidst thy truly." St. John 4:16-18*

God doesn't want to just bind up your broken heart and heal your wounds he wants you to learn what caused the broken heart and wound, and not repeat this episode again.

God want you to observe your last relationship or marriage and begin analyzing what mistakes you made and what went wrong. What principles and morals you compromised on that you shouldn't have. What pressures you gave into that you later regretted and what things you should have done that you didn't do.

Here are five reasons why Christians end up with broken hearts, broken relationships and divorces in marriage.

1. *Because saved people are in relationships with or marrying unsaved people.*

2. *Because saved people are in relationships with or*

marrying people out of character for them.

3. ***Because saved people are in relationships with or marrying people that are incompatible to them.***

4. ***Because God's people are just outright disobeying God's leading.***

5. ***Because saved people are marrying mainly for sexual, economic or status reasons.***

God wants to get you to the place in your life where you're ready for your true soul mate, however you can delay this time by disobedience and not seeking God in prayer. The scripture says; *"Then shall ye call upon me, and ye shall go and pray unto me, and I will hearken unto you." Jeremiah 29:12*

While you are waiting on God to bless you with your soul mate allow him to settle you and repair you. Let the potter wrought his work on the wheel of your life and yield to it so that when he brings your soul mate and you together, you will compliment each other and not frustrate each other.

"But the God of all grace, who hath called us unto his eternal glory by Christ Jesus, ***after that ye have suffered a while, make you perfect (repair you), stablish, strengthen, settle you.****" 1 Peter 5:10*

Realize that everything takes time but make it your business not to delay the time by your disobedience and refusal to seek the Lord. The scriptures says; *"To everything there is a season, and a time to every purpose under the heaven **(seasons and times don't last forever)**: A time to weep, **(you may be in a time of weeping as a result of broken relationships and broken promises)** and a time to laugh (**but*** *the time will come that your weeping shall turn to laughter because God has answered you in the joy of your heart); a time to mourn (the time of mourning may be upon you from the past), and a time to dance (but be encouraged for the time of dancing and praising God shall come upon you, the time of rejoicing and singing that your joy may be full); "* Ecclesiastes 3:1, 4, 5:20, St. John 16:24

The individual that keeps doing the same things is going to keep getting the same results, you cannot expect different results following the same pattern.

If you want a relationship like you've never had then you must do something that you've never done. You must seek God like you never have before and be watchful and observant like you never have before.

Refuse from this day forward to continue a pattern of broken relationships and broken promises, but decide that you will acknowledge God more than you ever have before in finding your soul mate.

*"But Seek ye first the kingdom of God, and his righteousness; and all these things (**relationship and marriage**) shall be added unto you." Matthew 6:33*

"Trust in the LORD with all thine heart; and lean not unto thine own understanding. In all thy ways acknowledge him, and he shall direct thy paths. Be not wise in thine own eyes: fear the LORD, and depart from evil. It shall be health to thy navel, and marrow to thy bones." Proverbs 3:5-8

God wants to free you from a life of broken relationships and broken promises and lead you in the right direction and on the right path so that you shall be brought together with your true soul mate by his divine wisdom and understanding.

3

Finding a Good Thing

"Whoso findeth a wife findeth a good thing, and obtaineth favour of the LORD. Houses and riches are the inheritance of fathers and a prudent wife is from the LORD."
Proverbs 18:22, 19:14

Since the scriptures emphasize that marriage is a good thing then why are there so many bad marriages with one out of two of all marriages ending in divorce? Obviously individuals have not found their good thing.

The reason there is such a high divorce rate is because individuals aren't marrying their soul mates but are marrying just another date. Throughout the Scriptures, we see many individuals that married their soul mates and the marriage lasted until death did them apart.

> We see the marriage of Adam and Eve. *Genesis 2:21-25, 3:20, 4:1*
> We see the marriage of Noah and his wife. *Genesis 6:8-9, 7:7, 13*
> We see the marriage of Abram and Sarai. *Genesis 11:29, 21:2*
> We see the marriage of Isaac and Rebekah. *Genesis 24:67*
> We see the marriage of Jacob and Rachel. *Genesis 29:28*
> We see the marriage of Moses and Zipporah. *Exodus 2:21*

There are many others that we could include here, but this gives you an idea of what happens when an individual is joined together with their soul mate versus being joined together with just another date. Every couple joined in holy matrimony isn't God's best choice for each other.

Also, we have an interesting portrayal of one of these individual that married someone, but the individual was not his soul mate but turned out to be just another date and the relationship was not sound.

Here we have the story of Jacob, who came to his uncle and after a time of fellowship, Jacob decided to remain with them for a month.

"And Laban had two daughters: the name of the elder was Leah, and the name of the younger was Rachel. Leah was tender eyed; but Rachel was beautiful and well favoured. **(There was also a physical attraction to Rachel)** *And Jacob loved Rachel;* **(she was his soul mate)** *and said, I will serve thee seven years for Rachel thy younger daughter.*

And Jacob served seven years for Rachel; and they seemed unto him but a few days, **for the love he had to her***. And Jacob said unto Laban, Give me my wife, for my days are fulfilled, that I may go in unto her.*

And Laban gathered together all the men of the place, and made a feast. And it came to pass in the evening, that he took Leah his daughter, and brought her to him; and he went in unto her.

And it came to pass that in the morning, behold, it was Leah: and he said to Laban, What is this that thou hast done unto me? Did not I serve with thee for Rachel? Wherefore then hast thou beguiled me?

And Laban said, It must not be so done in our country, to give the younger before the firstborn. Fulfill her week, and we will give thee this also for the service which thou shalt serve with me yet seven other years.

And Jacob did so, and fulfilled her week: and he gave him Rachel his daughter to wife also. **And he went in also unto Rachel, and he loved also Rachel more than Leah, and served with him yet seven other years***." Genesis 29:16-18, 20-23, 25-28, 30*

The point I want to make here is that Jacob had a unification of spirit and soul **with Rachel as well as a physical attraction that he did not have with Leah, and it was so powerful that he was willing to work an additional seven years (** *a total of 14 years)* **just to have her.**

In truth, he would not have worked seven days to have Leah because with her he had no unification of spirit and soul and no physical attraction; there was no true connection with her. Leah was not his soul mate she was in our terms just another date that he was tricked into and had to marry.

But Rachel was his soul mate and he knew it in a brief period of time for it was only after a month of being there that he told her father *"I will serve thee seven years for Rachel thy younger daughter, and Jacob loved Rachel." Genesis 29:18*

Jacob obviously had an inward witness and peace that Rachel was for him for he loved her greatly in so short a time that it did not take him years to know his love for her, he knew within a month's time. I once heard a gentlemen say *after fifteen years of marriage I've just really fallen in love with my wife,* how disheartening he should have been in love with her before he ever married her.

Jacob never loved Leah at all the scriptures even said that he hated Leah but he loved Rachel. *Genesis 29:31* Rachel was to Jacob a good thing and their marriage never ended in divorce.

God desires that every man find his good thing which is his soul mate, *for no other person can do for you what your soul mate can do for you,* to Jacob Leah was like night, but Rachel was like day.

God desires that every woman would have her soul mate and not marry just another date because that date cannot give to you on a human level what God has designed specifically for your soul mate to fulfill.

God is not telling you that your soul mate can fulfill the desire in your heart that only he can fill, but there is a place in your heart that God has put there for your soul mate to fill.

God said that it's not good that Adam be alone, not saying that God was not fulfilling Adam's need, but there was a place in Adam's heart and life that God had designed for a help meet to fill.

If you have a desire to find your soul mate and be married that desire is from God, for marriage is not something that you work up but it's a gift given by God not to everyone, but certainly to those that have a desire.

Paul, in speaking to the church at Corinth about marriage used himself as an example of an unmarried person that has no desire for marriage saying *"For I would that all men were even as I myself. But every man hath his proper gift of God, one after this manner, and another after that." 1 Corinthians 7:7* Stating that some have the gift of marriage from God and some don't.

Jesus stated that some people are eunuch saying *"For there are some eunuchs, which were so born of their mother's womb: and there are some eunuchs, which were made eunuchs of men: and there be eunuchs, which have made themselves eunuchs for the kingdom of heaven's sake. He that is able to receive it, let him receive it."* Matthew 19:12

The key verse here is *"He that is able to receive it, let him receive it."* The majority of individuals are not born from their mother's womb to be eunuchs the majority have a desire for marriage and to find their soul mate.

Those that have a desire for marriage and want to live righteous and holy before God need to find or be found by their good thing, their soul mate and have the celebration of love that God has designed for their lives.

4

Soul Mate Course

"Whoso findeth a wife findeth a good thing, and obtaineth favour of the LORD." Proverbs 18:22

This chapter may seem a bit unorthodox in reference to how to find or be found of your soul mate. Yet, this chapter is actually essential to helping you attract your soul mate God's way and allowing your life to flow according to God's destiny for you in relationships.

The word course is defined according to the dictionary as ***the way in which something progress or develops. A procedure adopted to deal with a situation. A direction followed or intended.***

In the book of Acts Paul talked about a course that he was following that would ultimately lead him on to victory and enable him to testify the gospel of the grace of God, saying, *"But none of these things move me, neither count I my life dear unto myself, so that I might **finish my course** with joy, and the ministry, which I have received of the Lord Jesus, to testify the gospel of the grace of God." Acts 20:24*

And in the book of Timothy he reiterated this again but from a different perspective, this time he was stating that he has **finished his course** and his reward is waiting, saying, *"I have fought a good fight, **I have finished my course**, I have kept the faith: Henceforth there is laid up for me a crown of righteousness, which the Lord, the righteous judge, shall give me at that day: and not to me only, but unto all them also that love his appearing." 2 Timothy 4:7-8*

Paul here was referring to a course that was laid out for him that if he followed would end up with great dividends on his part, but he had to follow the course in order to receive the rewards.

In every phase of life there are courses that can lead us on to victory and success in that particular area of life. However, many times we perish for a lack of knowledge of that course and when we don't know the course we proceed to make up our own course or a course taught to us by others that have not been successful.

In relationships we don't have many good examples, seeing that according to statistics 1 out of every 2 marriages end in divorce. And many other marriages that are not divorcing are remaining married for many other reasons beside love and because they have found their soul mate.

Well, in this book we will give you the Soul Mate Course that will enable you to not only find or be found of your soul mate but will equip you with that essential knowledge necessary for attracting the right person in your life.

We have organized this into two simple concepts to insure balance and understanding for the reader. We call them the **Soul Mate or Just Another Date Course** and the **Stairway to Soul Mate Success or Just Another Date disaster.**

These two concepts will give you an understanding of the process of how the Soul Mate and Just Another Date Course works and develops. The **Soul Mate or Just Another Date Course** shows you how things are done and the Stairway to Soul Mate Success or Just Another Date Disaster shows you what to do and what not to do.

The beautiful thing about these two concepts are that every person either follows one course or the other and both courses are designed to show you what can happen when its done right and what can happen when its done wrong.

Each stage on the circle of development will enable you to know whether to proceed further with the individual you're communicating with without sacrificing much of your time, money and energy.

However, if you try to get around the stages you will get off course and likely end up in disaster or off the path destined for success. If you only get to stage two on the Soul Mate Course with an individual and find out that this person is not your soul mate but just another date you have still successfully finished that course. Our objective with this is to get you on the course that will lead you to success in finding or being found of your soul mate. If you follow the procedure you will find the love of your life and enjoy the celebration of love that God has destined for you.

Soul Mate Course

The Stairway to Soul Mate Success

Soul Mate
True love and commitment. Compatiblity and inner peace abides here.

Friend
At this stage there is a bond of mutual affection established that has come as a result of spending quality time.

Date / Dating
DATE = To have a social appointment with one another. At this stage you want to get to know one another on a more social level.
DATING = To have a romantic appointment with one another. At this stage you want to get to know one another on a more personal and intimate level.

Acquaintance
This is a person that you slightly know. This person is one step above a stranger to you. This is a person that you are getting to know and it takes time to move from here. You can't go from this step to the next overnight. Many mistakenly think so and try to rush things to the next step.

The Right Way

The Soul Mate Course Defined

1. **Stranger** = This is your starting point in your endeavor to find or be found of your soul mate. The person that you come into contact with is first off a stranger to you, this is an unknown person that you come into contact with.

You may come into contact with this person in a variety of ways, to numerous to name all of the ways in detail but we will name a few. You may come in contact with this person by way of:

- *Going to the grocery store.*
- *Online dating.*
- *At Church.*
- *At a meeting.*
- *On the job.*
- *By introduction of someone else.*
- *And many other ways.*

In the beginning this person is a stranger to you an unknown person that you don't know.

2. **Acquaintance** = The next circle represents someone that you want to get to know. That stranger become someone that you want to spend time with to get to know about. Through **time** this will become someone that you know slightly.

The key here is that this person moves from being a stranger to becoming an acquaintance through the **process of time**. It doesn't happen over night but it happens as you **spend time** in talking with the person to get to know the person.

3. **Date** = After the process of time has developed and we will not put a stipulation on how long it will take for this to occur you will then move on to the next circle which represents a

date.

What we have omitted is the understanding of the word date and therefore we have been destroyed for our lack of knowledge. The word date is defined as a **social** or **romantic appointment.**

However, we have moved swiftly to a romantic appointment and have skipped over the first phase of dating which is simply a social appointment. The social appointments comes way before the romantic appointments and the social appointments is designed because we want to know this individual. It's simply a matter of wanting to know who this individual is.

4. **Dating** = This phase of the circle goes along with the dates aspects of the **Circle of Development.** Even though the word dating is not included there this is the time when you've put in many social appointments knowing the person that eventually it moves to dating or **romantic appointment.**

The social appointments will let you know through time whether or not to move it further on to romantic appointments. If the flow is good and the connections are there then you can move on to the romantic appointments. If you aren't feeling it in the social appointments then no need to move further with romantic appointments. In romantic appointments the two of you have a connection and you're really feeling each other and a bond is developing. Now when you go on a date the conversation changes from you or I to us. At this point the conversation moves from your or my future to our future together. Romantic appointments have nothing to do with sex at all (sex is something you want to keep out of your relationship before marriage, it simply confuses everything and God forbids it with unmarried people). *Acts 15:20, 29, 21:25, 1 Corinthians 6:13, 18, 7:2,*

10:8, Ephesians 5:3, Colossians 3:5, 1 Thessalonians 5:3
Romantic appointments gives you the opportunity to be together and bond spiritually, mentally and emotionally.

5. **Friends** = This phase of the circle comes after you have spent time with the person in knowing the individual and much have been discussed and revealed by the both of you.

This is the phase where a bond of mutual affection has been established between the two of you. This is a really serious phase and you're really feeling the individual and they're really feeling you. You know this person and they know you and the bond is so incredible, it's like you have known this person all your life and there is a spiritual and soul (mental) connection. You enjoy being in the presence of this person and the feeling is mutual.

6. **Soul Mate** = This is the final phase of the circle and you know that this is the person that you want to spend the rest of your life with. Not only do you know this person but they know you and this has become a person not that you can live with but a person that you **(figuratively speaking)** cannot live without. This is the person that you will marry and enjoy the celebration of love that can only be found when you meet your soul mate.

Just Another Date Course

"There is a way which seemeth right unto a man, but the end thereof are the ways of death." Proverbs 14:12

Our beginning scripture speaks to us concerning a way that seems right but at the end of that way we find the way of death. In our two analogies of courses we have presented to you first off the **Soul Mate Course,** and now we present to you the **Just Another Date Course.**

One course will lead you on the way of life in relationships and the other course leads you to the way of death. Sadly, many are taking the way of death or the **Just Another Date Course** and this course will ultimately lead them back to a life of singleness.

We have already explained according to the scriptures how Paul had a course and finished it. He proceeded with the course which lead him to life, if he would have gotten off that course he would have ended up in the way of death.

This **Just Another Date Course** is the course we want to deter you from following, for the end thereof is the way of a dead relationship. As we explain to you the **Circle of Catastrophe** and the **Stairway to Disaster** this is the route we want to derail you from.

These two concepts likewise will give you an understanding of the process of how the **Just Another Date Course** works and develops. The **Circle of Catastrophe** shows you *what most individuals do* and the **Stairway to Disaster** shows you *how most people do it.*

Both of these concepts are arranged to let you know what the end result will be when these methods are followed. Our objective here is to reveal to you the outcome of pursuing such methods that will eventually end in death.

Just Another Date Course

Stairway to Just Another Date Disaster

Back to Singleness

This final step has led them back to where they started. Singleness!

Disconnection

A this stage these two individuals have gotten off course. The disconnection has put a wedge between them and caused them to go their seperate ways.

Promiscuous

At this stage the individuals has become sexually involved with each other even though they don't really know each other.

Dating

The tragedy of this first step is the individual has skipped over the three most important steps in establishing a relationship. They have omitted, Getting Acquainted, Having the Social Appointments to establish the interests of each other. Also, they have omitted the Friends stage in order to establish a mutual bond with each other.

The Wrong Way

The Circle of Catastrophe Defined

1. **Stranger** = This is your starting point in your endeavor to find or be found of your soul mate. The person that you come into contact with is first off a stranger to you, this is an unknown person that you come into contact with.

You may come into contact with this person in a variety of ways, to numerous to name all the many ways in detail but we will name a few. You may come in contact with this person by the way of:

• *Going to the grocery store.*
• *Online dating.*
• *At Church.*
• *At a meeting.*
• *On the job.*
• *By introduction of someone else.*
• *And many other ways.*

2. **Dating** = One reason this is called the **Circle of Catastrophe** is because on this course the individual has omitted some things of vital importance in establishing a sound relationship. If you will observe the chart you will notice that they have skipped the ***acquaintance, date*** and the ***friend*** phases of the circle in accordance to the **Circle of Development** chart.

They have went right to the dating stage which is defined as setting romantic appointments with the individual. (Go *back and read in the* **Circle of Development Defined** *the importance of the* **Date** *and social appointments).*

When the **date** phase is omitted you have not given yourself time to know who this individual is, yet you have already begin talking about us and our future together. When you skip vital steps you're setting yourself up for failure.

3. **Promiscuous** = In this phase the two individuals have become intimately involved sexually and have given themselves to each other even though they really don't know each other.

This phase has much pleasure in the way of physical intimacy and sexual stimulation. It satisfies your flesh but it does not mean that you have found true intimate involvement with your soul mate.

It will not produce a true bond of mutual affection toward each other. Most of the time it confuses things and gives you a false reading and understanding of the person that you're with. It feels good but it's not real and it will eventually phase out. This is not the best method and course designed to find or be found of your soul mate therefore it will be short lived and still echo a void in you that this is not the your true soul mate. When sex becomes a lifestyle in your relationship it really confuses things and many times takes it to the next level.

4. **Disconnection** = In this phase you will discover that the individual you thought was your soul mate turned out to be just another date. However, you have given of yourselves to each other and now the two of you have to go your separate ways taking with you a broken heart and broken promises.

You have just encountered the **Circle of Catastrophe** and it's ultimate goal is to lead you right back to your starting point of **Just Another Date.**

5. **Just Another Date** = Here you are once again right back where you started, back to singleness and you have wasted much time, money and energy because you have allowed

yourself to follow the Circle of Catastrophe and the Stairway to Disaster.

Get out of this circle and do it right and follow the course that is designed to bring you success and happiness. The course that will save you time, money and energy and enable you to find your soul mate in the 21st century and experience the wholeness that God has designed for your life.

5

Friend to Friend

"This is my beloved, and this is my friend, O daughters of Jerusalem." Song of Solomon 5:16

A friend is defined in Webster's dictionary as *one attached to another by respect or affection. One who supports or favors someone or something.*

One of the missing ingredients in relationships today is friendship, many times individuals become lovers sexually even before they become friends. Not realizing that intimacy isn't going to make a person truly respect or become affectionate toward them, nor will it cause an individual to support or favor them.

The scriptures has many things to say concerning a friend that will enlighten you in your understanding of how it relates to relationships when you have found a true friend.

• A *friend loveth at all times. Proverbs 17:17*

• *A man that hath friends must shew himself friendly: and there is a friend that sticketh closer than a brother. Proverbs 18:24*

• *Faithful are the wounds of a friend. Proverbs 27:6*

• *Ointment and perfume rejoice the heart: so doth the sweetness of a man's friend by hearty counsel. Proverbs 27:9*

- *Greater love hath no man than this, that a man lay down his life for his friends. Ye are my friends, if ye do whatsoever I command you. Henceforth I call you not servants; for the servant knoweth not what his lord doeth: but I have called you friends; for all things that I have heard of my Father I have made known unto you. John 15:13-15*

If you fail to become friends before you become seriously involved with one another you will not be in a relationship with someone that will love you at all times, but will only love you conditionally.

In order for the two of you to become friends with each other you both must first show yourself friendly towards each other in words, deed and in truth. For if you can't show yourself friendly then you will not have an individual in your corner that will stick with you through thick and thin, good and bad, richer or poorer and till death do you part.

If you have only encountered dates, the one thing that has been void in your relationships is true and lasting friendship. A true friend will not only tell you the truth even if it hurts, but will also bring you pleasantness and hearty counsel and good advice when needed.

A true friend because they are true will not demand that things always be their way, but will be willing to lay down their life *(or manner of thinking and doing)* in order to keep harmony and peace in the friendship. A true friend will not keep things away from you, but will be willing to disclose and expose themselves to you knowing that they can do this in confidence for you are their friend. Jesus said *"Henceforth I call you not servants; for the servant knoweth not what his lord doeth: but I have called you friends; for all things I have heard of my Father I have made known unto you."* John

15:15

True friendship takes time, love can happen quickly, but true love grows and develops as it gives space for friendship to mature it and make it fruitful. When true love is enveloped in true friendship then you have encountered a relationship that can only be described according to love exemplified in the scriptures.

- *Love suffereth long, and is kind;*
- *Love envieth not;*
- *Love vaunteth not itself, is not puffed up;.*
- *Love doth not behave itself unseemly;*
- *Love seeketh not her own, is not easily provoked and thinketh no evil;*
- *Love rejoiceth not in iniquity, but rejoiceth in the truth;*
- *Love beareth all things, believeth all things, hopeth all things, endureth all things.*
- *Love never fails. 1 Corinthians 13: 4-8a*

True friendship will respect one another's morals and decisions, it will not ask one to do wrong when the other has stipulated boundaries and beliefs. Let me give you an example: If you're in a relationship with someone and you tell them that because of your Christian belief and relationship with Christ you don't desire to engage in sex outside of marriage or any sexual activities, a true friend will respect this.

An individual that's not a true friend will try to persuade you with many reasons and excuses why the two of you should engage in sex or sexual activities even though they know how you feel about the situation. Remember, the definition of friend according to Webster is *one attached to another by respect or affection. One who supports or favors someone or something.*

You don't want excuses, reasons or persuasions from one that is supposed to be your friend, you want respect, affection, support and favor and this you will get from a true friend and this is the type of person that can be your soul mate.

When you find this type of friend you will find your ***rayah (Strong's Concordance ref 7453),*** this is the Hebrew word in scripture that is defined as ***companion, friend, husband, wife and lover.***

In your endeavor to find and be found of your soul mate don't settle for less than your **rayah**, for in your rayah you will find a *friend that loves at all times, a friend that sticks closer than a brother and a friend that will lay down their life for you*. With this person you will enjoy a celebration of love that comes when you have found your soul mate and not just another date.

6

Are You Attracting Your Soul Mate

"The man who finds a wife find a good thing. She is a blessing to him from the LORD." Proverbs 18:22 (NIV)

Proverbs states that a man that finds a wife, therefore there are men that's looking for us women to become their wife. As the man is looking for his blessing and gift, my question to you is are you attracting the man of God that you're seeking?

If you are seeking or looking for a husband that means you are not attracting your mate for God has not equipped you to do such a thing.

* *Rule number one, men are equipped to track, we are created to be found.*

Many of God's women have stated, *I can't find a man* or *men are not attracted to me.* One thing that God placed within men is the ability to be attracted to the opposite sex. If we are not attracting what God has placed in the man then as women we need to check out what is hindering us from being attracted.

Let me give you a personal testimony to show that a man is equipped to track and we are equipped to be found. One Monday afternoon in January, I was coming from a midmorning work meeting that was supposed to be just a temporary meeting in which we were not required to dress up as we do for normal work.

So I decided to put on some sweat pants and just pull my hair back in a ponytail. My plan was to go to work for the meeting and run to the store for some groceries, and afterwards come straight home because I had some more reading and writing that I need to get caught up on.

While I was in the store minding my own business and not even feeling attractive, I looked up as I was walking across the isle and saw this young man. There was nothing special about him, but I had a witness in my spirit about this man. I kept walking and went to look at the books in the book isle.

I wanted to see if my favorite author had any new books out. As I was looking at the books, I looked up and the young man was looking down the isle, I continue to look at the books and he continued to come closer. I looked at him and gave a friendly smile, and he proceeded past me as I continued to look at the books.

Sisters, this young man proceeded around the isle about two times, then I said to myself this man is trying to get my attention. About the third time he gained enough courage to ask me if I had a moment, so I kindly said yes.

So the young man began to talk to me telling me who he was and that he was looking for his soul mate. God gave me this divine appointment to give witness to the writing of this book and to show me in experience how he has made men equipped to track and women are equipped to be found.

I thought that was very awesome in relations to the timing of the writing of the book and the revealing of how God works. But remember I said not everyone that tracks you is for you. I also knew by being polite, having a godly conversation and the things which we are teaching here that he was definitely not my soul mate. Ok, that's enough about that keep-reading.

One thing I have learned and come to understand from renowned author and good friend Dexter Jones is that a man has a right to seek whom he desires.

As an example, if you are interested in a man and he chooses another woman it's ok, because he knows what he is seeking after. Every man does not have the same type of desire in a woman. Not every man desires a petite woman, nor does every man desire a full figured woman.

The desire is in the heart of the man, but one thing is certain, every man desires his soul mate. Every man desires a good woman and an attractive woman.

Yes, contrary to what you feel or have been told you are an attractive woman. There is a man who is seeking you and your beauty.

This chapter is about allowing your beauty to attract your soul mate and that beauty is both within and without. Outward beauty alone will not attract you to your true soul mate, but a combination of inward and outward beauty will draw you to the one destined to be your soul mate and life mate.

Proverbs said a man that finds a wife, but you have to remember that you are a woman before you become a wife. So in reality a man is looking for a woman to become his wife, but he wants a woman that is a good thing and is a blessing from the Lord.

Are you a good thing?
Are you a blessing from the Lord?
Are you ready for God to expose you to your soul mate?

YOU ARE BEAUTIFUL AND UNIQUE

To my sisters that are dealing with what I call silent cries, those tears that you shed that no one knows you are shedding but God and you. Let me define how those silent cries affect your life and circumstances.

On one occasion, a student of mine informed me that I had hurt her feelings. I said "sweetie how did I do that"? She said, "You asked me was I pregnant". On that particular morning my students and I were just relaxing and getting ready for the morning and when she walked in the classroom I said "are you pregnant" and she said "no".

So as the day went on I was informed that she was crying. I went to her and asked her, "Baby why you are crying"? She said, "You hurt my feelings".

At this point I was a little shocked, so I asked what did I do. She said, "You hurt my feelings by asking me was I pregnant". But I have learned compassion for people and what one person can handle may be devastating to another.

She said, "I thought you were saying that I was fat", but I never said anything about her weight *(also she is not fat)*. She said I am very sensitive about my weight.

Yes, I apologized, but also gained great insight about the silent cries. Her silent cry was her weight and the fat she imagined her self to be.

So the silent cries are anything that the enemy Satan can use to attach himself to in order to make the individual feel inadequate and lower their self-esteem.

The silent cries are strongholds in our lives that Satan uses and its power is to keep us from believing that we are beautiful. 1 Peter 5:9 says, *"Whom resist steadfast in the faith, knowing that the same afflictions are accomplished in your brethren that are in the world."*

No matter what body shape or size you are, you and I are still created beautiful because we are created in God's image. Genesis 1:27 *"So God created man in his own image, in the image of God created he him; male and female created he them."*

So if someone doesn't like the way you are created then they don't like the image of God and they're definitely not your soul mate or life mate. A dissatisfied person will surely be tempted to find satisfaction elsewhere, but an individual that is satisfied is complete, content and gratified, for he or she has found what meets their requirements and desires.

As a woman you have to be satisfied first with yourself, here is an exercise for you to do. Get in front of a mirror and look at yourself from head to toe and say, *"I am created in the image and likeness of God. I am beautiful because God created me."*

In order for anyone else to accept you and love you, you must first accept and love yourself. Love all of who God created you to be and that love you have for yourself will begin to exude from you and others will sense that, and you will be found by your soul mate.

The reason why the devil doesn't like you and tries to keep you wrapped up in your silent cries is because you remind him of God and when he sees you he sees the image and likeness of the Godhead.

But the devil is a liar and the truth is not in him. He was a liar and murderer from the beginning and the father of it. John 8:44. Do not let the devil belittle you and keep you wrapped up in your silent cries, but tell that devil that you are a child of God and you refuse to accept his words.

You must then come to the conclusion that God is for you and therefore who can be against you, and become adamant in telling yourself that you are beautiful and unique. And right now God is orchestrating the destinies of you and your ideal soul mate so that the both of you will be at the right place at the right time to meet one another for a lifetime of celebration and love.

What God Desires For His Girls To Know, And What A Man Wants From A Woman

As Founder of The Real Women Ministries, I have the awesome privilege to hear the desires of God's Real Women. Here is a nugget about real women. Real Women are what I call Precious Miraculous Sisters or (P.M.S.), which means that we are truly amazing, even when we don't feel like we are, we're still amazing to God. Real Women are hand picked by God.

1. *Real Women continually strive to be conformed to his image.*
2. *Real Women are endowed with gifts and abilities to perform good works for Him.*
3. *Real Women are blessed to be a blessing.*
4. *Real Women are fruitful in carrying out the gospel.*
5. *Real Women believe in the name of Jesus Christ and signs and wonders follow her wherever she goes.*
6. *Real Women operate in her God given authority.*
7. *Real Women receive her nourishment from the Word of God.*

8. *Real Women strive to please God and Him only at all times.*
9. *Real Women are aware of the mission placed before her from God.*
10. *Real Women can do all things through Christ that strengthens her.*
11. *Real Women are fully developed mature Christian woman, who stands naked and unashamed in God's presence because Christ is their righteousness.*

Yet, as Real Women we desire our ideal soul mate. Not just any mate, but a Real Man of the Kingdom of God. In order to be found by such a man we must began to listen to the voice of God and allow the Holy Spirit to teach us all things.

In John 14:26 it says, *"But the Comforter, which is the Holy Ghost, whom the Father will send in my name, he shall teach you all things, and bring all things to your remembrance, (some of the things he want to teach us as women is how to be a woman of God, he wants to teach us the wisdom keys on how to be a woman fit for the Real Men of The Kingdom of God)."*

- *Men are looking for a wise woman. Proverbs 14:1 says, "a wise woman builds her house, while a foolish women tears hers down by her own efforts. A woman who is sophisticated and is confident in the God that is in her." The Living Bible*

- *A woman who knows how to exhibit common sense, a woman of great learning and one that speaks to and into her mate a good word in due season.*

- *A woman who knows that a virtuous woman is one that knows how important a soft answer is to her mate and those around her.*

- *A woman that knows how to be gracious. Proverbs 11:16, "A gracious woman retaineth honour." She is characterized by kindness and warm courtesy, tact and propriety (one that responds to insult with gracious humor), merciful and compassionate in nature, characterized by charm, beauty and gracefulness, elegance and good taste.*

- *A woman that knows who she is. Real men are looking for a woman that has confidence in who she is and isn't moved by what other people around her may think or say about her. She is a Real Woman because she isn't afraid of constructive criticism. Proverbs 15:32 states, "If you profit from constructive criticism you will be elected to the wise men's hall of fame. But to reject criticism is to harm yourself and your own best interest." The Living Bible*

- *A woman of high standards, one that will not lower her standards because of her flesh or because her biological clock is ticking.*

- *A Real Woman knows that her body belongs to the Lord, she is anointed of God, she is a jewel and her price is far above rubies, therefore she will not allow her body to be tampered with for she has been purchased at a very costly price, the precious blood of the Lamb.*

- *A Real Woman knows that until she is married, her intimate desire will be to the Father, she knows that being intimate is a spiritual thing and not a natural thing. Any male that desires her has to go to the*

Father and purchase her rightly from the throne of heaven.

- *Real Women know that the cost of being intimate naturally outside the bonds of marriage will leave her wounded, feeling rejected and mistreated, it promotes low self-esteem or low self-image. She knows that natural intimacy outside of God's ordained plan will truly hinder her spiritual growth, but as long as she is obedient to God that is where her true wealth lies.*

- *Real Women fully understand what 2 Corinthians 6:14 says, "Don't be teamed up with those who do not love the Lord, for what do the people of God have in common with the people of Sin? How can light live with darkness?"* **The Living Bible**

- *A Real Woman knows that she has to have more in common with the opposite sex than her sexual desires. Here is something that the Spirit of the Lord shared with me that helps me and I liberally share it with others. I actually picture that God has to turn his face from me if I allow myself to be caught up with sexual activities, because God cannot look on sin. Also within that moment of pleasure the enemy can move in and bring forth a pregnancy that will expose what I have been doing. Or even worse will move in with diseases that will lead to death. The act may be fun and pleasurable, but exposure is not. You have to ask yourself, is that moment of pleasure worth the scars, exposure, rejection or condemnation that will come upon you?*

- *A Real Woman knows that she is accountable for what she does with her body and that sex outside of*

marriage is sin and even if she doesn't contract a sexual disease she will still transfer different spirits, which will attach themselves to her and create bondage that may seem almost impossible to break.

In conclusion, will the Real Women of God stand up and take your rightful place, refusing to take down or lower your standard for anyone. For you know that you are indeed God's leading lady and Precious Daughter.

7

Your Ideal Soul Mate

"Who can find a virtuous woman? For her price is far above rubies. The heart of her husband doth safely trust in her, so that he shall have no need of spoil. She will do him good and not evil all the days of her life." Proverbs 31:10-12

In view of the staggering divorce rate, we can conclude that the majority of individuals have not found their ideal soul mate but have married individuals that were just another date.

I must admit that my life has become a part of the statistic of the staggering divorce rate, the things which I now understand I did not understand then I wish I had this book in the beginning it could have saved me a lot of broken relationships and broken promises.

One bit of vital information I must share is that I now understand that my marriage didn't work not because either of us was bad or had evil intentions, it didn't work because there was too many incompatible things between the two of us.

We are both Christian people and you would think that would be enough to make it good, but that only gives us unification of spirit which is not enough to make a happy, sound and enduring relationship and marriage. We both love God and believe in doing the right thing, but this is not enough and sad to say that many individuals before the year is out will marry with this same mind set.

Like some of you, I have been in relationships after my marriage at the beginning it seemed as if all was well and we were destined for a life of bliss and romance.

I thought for sure I had finally found my soul mate and my life long search was finally over. I no longer had to be in the dating game all that was now over for I had finally found the one that I had been looking for.

Each day seemed to get better and better as we drew closer emotionally to each other, this just seemed right and time was on our side and would only bring us closer together.

There were even some unification of spirit and soul in each of the relationships.

Some of the relationships lasted for several months and each of the individuals were wonderful Christian ladies that loved the Lord just as I love the Lord.

Things were talked about and even some plans were made as to a future together, feelings were high and even a commitment was established in some case.

Yet as time went on, it begin to be evident that we were not soul mates as we had previously thought but were two individuals that were just on another date. As I analyze these relationships I notice that there was always **the voice of doubt** in the back of my mind and heart letting me know that this was not the true one, yet I blocked it out.

The relationships ended and we both went our separate ways taking with us broken hearts and broken promises looking to God to heal the broken heart and bind up the wound.

After this last relationship it was then that God blessed me to discover the difference and truth between finding your soul mate and just experiencing another date.

There were many things that happened between the time of my last date and discovering how to find my ideal soul mate that made all the difference.

1. *I learned what I did that I shouldn't have done on my last dates.*

2. *I learned what to look for in the next person that I overlooked prior.*

3. *I learned to be more spirit conscious and to acknowledge God in a greater way than I ever had before.*

4. *I learned to not be so focused on the physical first but look first of all at the spirit of the individual.*

5. *I learned also that even though the spirit of the individual may be very good; was it good for me and my character and personality, was there a connection there that drew me mightily and based mainly on a spiritual knowing?.*

6. *Was this a person that I could not live (figuratively speaking) without and not someone that I could live with?*

7. *Also, this time I must allow God to help me find the person to come into my life instead of me trying to help God find my soul mate, by simply applying the principles and truths you will learn in the next chapter.*

Well I never believed in love at first sight because you have to establish some type of communication with the person to get to know the person first. Nor did I believe in love in a brief period of time. Yet, I have sense enough to know that there are always exceptions to every rule. One exception is that there can be an immediate witness and peace in your spirit that the individual is to be your soul mate and life partner.

For many scriptures accentuate this truth saying *"For as many as are led (Governed) by the Spirit of God, they are the sons of God." Romans 8:14*

"But ye have an unction from the Holy One, and ye know all things. But the anointing which ye have received of him abideth in you, and ye need not that any man teach you: but as the same anointing teacheth you of all things, and is truth, and is no lie, and even as it hath taught you, ye shall abide in him." 1 John 2:20, 27

"But while he thought on these things, behold, the angel of the Lord appeared unto him in a dream, saying, Joseph, thou son of David, fear not to take unto thee Mary thy wife: for that which is conceived in her is of the Holy Ghost. Then Joseph being raised from sleep did as the angel of the Lord had bidden him, and took unto him his wife." Matthew 1:20,24

"The LORD God of heaven, which took me from my father's house, and from the land of my kindred, and which spake unto me, and that sware unto me, saying Unto thy seed will I give this land; he shall send his angel before thee, and thou shalt take a wife unto my son from thence." Genesis 24:7

"And he said, O LORD God of my master Abraham, I pray thee, send me good speed this day, and shew kindness unto my master Abraham. Behold, I stand here by the well of water; and the daughters of the men of the city come out to draw water: And let it come to pass, that the damsel to whom

I shall say, Let down thy pitcher, I pray thee, that I may drink; and she shall say, Drink, and I will give thy camels drink also: let the same be she that thou hast appointed for thy servant Isaac; and thereby shall I know that thou hast shewed kindness unto my master. And it came to pass, before he had done speaking that, behold Rebekah came out, who was born to Bethuel, son of Milcah, the wife of Nahor, Abraham's brother, with her pitcher upon her shoulder." Genesis 24:12-15

The servant got the wife for Abraham's son Isaac just as Abraham had predicted and **it was not a task or painstaking effort.** He acknowledged God and God through his divine understanding and wisdom orchestrated the whole scenario and made it a success.

Dear reader, God knows you better than you know yourself and he knows the exact individual that will satisfy and fulfill the place that he has left open in your heart for your soul mate to fill.

Truly, there are certain aspects of a soul mate that should apply to all individuals; one thing in particular is that the relationship must begin on a sound spiritual basis.

1 *You must connect with the individual from the heart first and not the head.*

- *There must be sincerity, honesty, kindness, integrity and respect.*

- *You must not seek a mate for economic or social positions.*

- *You must not seek a mate for dependence of any kind*

you should be complete in Christ and not seeking a mate to fulfill the desire that only God can fill.

2 *You should have a relationship with Christ yourself first and love him because as a man if you don't know how to love Jesus you will never know how to love your mate. Ephesians 5:25-28, 33*

As a woman, if you don't know how to submit and be subject to God you will never be able to submit and be subject to your mate. Ephesians 5:22, 24

With this as a premise and foundation, I figured I was now ready to find my soul mate, yet God took me one step further so that the eyes of my understanding would be enlightened so I would know my soul mate when we met.

He taught me that I first had to condition my mind as well as my heart so that my mind could think the thoughts essential to bringing the soul mate that was to be my help meet into my world.

Just as others are presently thinking, the thoughts that were dominating my mind were thoughts that were not attracting to me my soul mate but was attracting to me just more dates while repelling from me my ideal soul mate.

The difference between the individual that will meet their soul mate and the individual that will continue to go on just another date are the thoughts that dominate their thinking about finding their soul mate.

You cannot wish, hope, desire and pray to meet your soul mate and then have thoughts of just another date dominating your thought life. How will this date turn out, will I ever meet the right person, how long will I have to go through this are all men (women) the same.

Either one thought pattern or the other will dominate your mind and produce results in accordance with the dominating thoughts you're thinking.

The scripture says *"For as he thinketh in his heart, so is he:" Proverbs 23:7.* You can't think one way and expect another way to come forth. The thoughts you're sowing in your mind you will reap in your life and there's no way around it. You will have and become what you think.

These dominating thoughts have a direct correlation and connection with the things that you are currently experiencing in your dating life.

You must come into the knowledge that your thoughts are what you will have and become. There is no exception to this rule, you will have in your life the dominating thoughts that you're thinking.

Rather those thoughts are just another date. Thoughts of continuous broken relationships and broken promises. Or thoughts of finding your ideal soul mate.

There is a universal law in the realm of the mind that works the same for all mankind, that law is **"like attracts like," "cause and effect," "what you sow, you will reap,"** and **"everything produces after its kind." Galatians 6: 7-8, Genesis 1:11-12**

An apple tree cannot produce oranges nor can a pecan tree produce plums every tree only produces after its kind. Luke 6:43-44

If you have daily dominating thoughts of "this is just another date, how will this date turn out, will I ever meet the right person, how long will I have to go through this or all men (women) are the same", this is the only thing you can ever receive.

"For as he thinketh in his heart, so is he." Proverbs 23:7 As he continues to think so he continues to be. However, if you have daily dominating thoughts of "I shall meet my ideal soul mate, God is now directing the path of my soul mate and I to each other, a prudent wife is from the Lord, God has blessed me to find my ideal soul mate", then this is the only thing that you can receive.

If the dominating thoughts of your mind has been the former negative way of thinking don't be dismayed, for the individual that begins to think spiritual and positive thoughts had to start those thoughts at some time and some place.

Today is your time, where you are right now is your place.

Now is the time to change your way of thinking and doing and begin to look toward the future with faith and hope that God is for you and wants you to find your ideal soul mate.

Now is the time to begin having dominating thoughts that will work for you instead of against you, thoughts that will attract your ideal soul mate instead of repelling them. The scriptures reveal to us what you need to do to think your way into a life of success, increase and prosperity in any area saying:

"Finally, brethren, whatsoever things are true, whatsoever things are honest, whatsoever things are just, whatsoever things are pure, whatsoever things are lovely, whatsoever things are of good report; if there be any virtue, and if there be any praise, think on these things." Philippians 4:8

Now I must ask you, is there any thing true, honest, just, pure, lovely, of good report, of virtue and of praise in thinking thoughts of *"how will this date turn out, when will I ever meet the right person, how long do I have to go through this, all men (women) are the same."* If your answer is no, then stop it because you're continually setting yourself up for a fall.

THOUGHTS CREATES CIRCUMSTANCES

The thoughts that dominate your mind have a direct effect on your circumstances. Man is not a creature of conditions, but instead creates his conditions by his dominating thoughts.

The person that continually goes on just another date has created these circumstances by their dominating thoughts.

All mankind will eventually have and become that which they secretly think about whether it's just another date or finding their soul mate.

The dominating thoughts of their mind that's hidden from others attract to them the environment and circumstances which their thoughts secretly longs for, whether good or bad.

THOUGHTS CREATES IMAGES

As the thoughts are passed down, so is the next level of living that seals the deal unless you break the pattern. The next level of living that's passed down is called imagery.

The dominating thoughts over time have formed a picture or image of your relationship life. This image and picture over time in return creates your circumstances.

What I want you to understand dear reader is this:

The image that you consistently hold in your mind will produce for you according to the image held.

> If you hold a continual image that God is directing the path of my soul mate and I to each other, a prudent wife is from the Lord, God has blessed me to find a good thing, and see yourself with your soul mate God will use that image to bring it to pass.

The word "image" is the root word of "imagination". The Hebrew definition of the word imagination is **"the squeezing into shape that which is out of shape to mold into a form, to frame.**

The imagination that comes from the thoughts you're thinking shapes a picture in your mind of those thoughts and molds those thoughts into a form or frame that's with you consistently. Whether negative or positive it's framed and formed into your mind.

The Greek definition of imagination means **"to take an inventory, conscience thought."** The proper imagination is vital to finding your ideal soul mate. Your imagination can either steer you toward finding your soul mate or repel you from your soul mate and your soul mate from you.

The Greek definition of image is defined as **"a likeness, a profile, representation or resemblance."**

The dominating thought of your mind causes an image that creates a likeness, a profile, a representation and resemblance in your outer circumstances.

THOUGHTS CREATES LIFESTYLES

Those dominating thoughts whether positive or negative will soon advance you to the final level of living. A level that produces such a stronghold on an individual that it will create a continual lifestyle according to those dominating thoughts.

Let your thoughts create the lifestyle that you envision. The lifestyle of not just another date, but of finding your ideal soul mate. For your outer circumstances will reflect your inner thoughts.

8

Attracting Your Soul Mate

"Draw me, we will run after thee, I am my beloved's and his desire is toward me. I am my beloved's, and my beloved is mine." Song of Solomon 1:4, 7:10, 6:3

In order to attract your ideal soul mate you must first of all know what type of soul mate you desire to have. The ideal soul mate for you is one that the two of you will blend perfectly together. Your ideal soul mate is one where the two of you have a shared purpose, with the capacity to enable each other to develop and grow spiritually, emotionally, physically and mentally.

It doesn't mean that the individual is perfect without flaw or fault, but he or she is perfect for you. However, that same individual that blends perfect with you may be a disastrous relationship with someone else; this doesn't mean that the person is bad only they're not right for someone else.

We have to learn that not everyone will blend perfectly with us no matter how good we may see ourselves. It's not really a reflection on you in particular; it's just a red light that this is not a go between the two of you.

If a person is not a go then don't try to force it and make it a go. You cannot make someone attractive to you that feels no chemistry between the two of you.

One of the things we want to teach you here is how to let God order your steps more and thereby reduce the number of dates that you will go on. The main way of doing this is by acknowledging God more in your choices and decisions when it come to dates.

This is done in one way as you pray to the Father and ask him to direct your steps. The scriptures says, *"Trust in the LORD with all thine heart; and lean not unto thine own understanding. In all thy ways acknowledge him, and he will direct thy paths." Proverbs 3:5-6*

Some experts believe that you shouldn't focus on asking God to help you find a mate, but you should focus more on establishing a relationship with God and finding your purpose in life.

We don't agree with all of this because it's partial truth, but not all truth and partial truth is more dangerous than no truth at all. Partial truth has the tendency to make you believe that you're doing the right thing yet it fails to produce the results because the other part(s) of the truth is missing.

When the experts make such a statement, they spiritualize the scriptures while omitting the part that can bring forth the answer and produce results.

To say to single men and women that are seeking to find their soul mate **"you should focus more on establishing a relationship with God and finding your purpose in life"** sounds real spiritual, but it lack substance, results and the whole truth.

True the scripture says, *"But seek ye first the kingdom of God, and his righteousness; and all these things (your soul mate, marriage) shall be added unto you." Matthew 6:33*

We agree wholeheartedly with that portion of their statement because the scriptures say the same thing in essence. But what the experts fail to realize here is that if there is a first something there is also a second something and third something.

As we seek first the kingdom of God and make establishing a relationship with him priority number one and even make finding our purpose in life priority number two nowhere does God tell us not to ask him for priority number three.

As a matter of fact, Jesus opened up the floodgates wide and said *"Therefore I say unto you, **What things soever ye desire**, when ye pray, **(meaning that I can ask him for whatever I desire it doesn't only have to be a closer walk with God and help me find my purpose, but it can also be help me find my soul mate for I desire to be married)** believe that ye receive them, and ye shall have them." Mark 11:24*

And then he goes even further and says, *"If ye shall ask any thing in my name, I will do it." John 14:14 "If ye abide in me, and my words abide in you, ye shall ask what ye will, and it shall be done unto you." John 15:7*

"And all things (cars, homes, clothes, money, finding your soul mate, marriage, all of these fall in the "things" category) whatsoever ye shall ask in prayer, believing, ye shall receive." Matthew 21:22

Why is God so eager to answer our prayers and give us the things that we desire in life? Let the scriptures speak for themselves: *"Hitherto have ye asked nothing in my name: ask, and ye shall receive, **that your joy may be full."** St. John 16:24.* God knows that if you have the gift of marriage and you have a desire to be married, to withhold marriage from you would deprive you of the fullness of joy in this life.

Yes, we need to make focusing on a relationship with God priority number one and finding our purpose and assignment in life a priority, but we do not have to omit asking him also to help us find our soul mate.

Deep Calleth Unto the Deep

"Deep calleth unto the deep at the noise of thy waterspouts: all thy waves and thy billows are gone over me." Psalm 42:7

The longing that you have in your heart and spirit for your soul mate your soul mate also has a longing in their heart and spirit for you.

The deep in them is calling for the deep in you.

The yearning in you is calling for the yearning in them.

The desire in them is calling for the desire in you.

Having the gift of marriage within you and then having that gift fulfilled is part of living the joyous life; for there will always be a missing link and yearning if you are compelled to be forever living the single life which you do not want to live.

It is the will of God for you to find or be found of your soul mate and enjoy marriage life; the fact that you have the desire is proof that the gift is operating and that God does want you to find your ideal soul mate and fulfill it by marriage.

The desire itself is an expression and sign within you that God in his wisdom has created and empowered you to fulfill this expression.

The person that is a eunuch has no real desire to find a soul mate nor for marriage, there is no expression seeking any fulfillment.

And when the desire for a soul mate and marriage is strong, this in itself is evidence and confirmation that the thing that you're seeking should be fulfilled, and only requires knowing how to find your soul mate and finding them God's way.

God is not against you desiring to find or be found of your soul mate and be married. The word of God affirms this throughout various scriptures saying;

"For I would that all men were even as I myself. But every man has his proper gift of God, one after this manner, and another after that. I say therefore to the unmarried and widows, It is good for them if they abide even as I. But if they cannot contain, let them marry: for it is better to marry than to burn." 1 Corinthians 7:7-9, "But and if thou marry, thou hast not sinned; and if a virgin marry, she hath not sinned. Nevertheless such shall have trouble in the flesh: but I spare you." 1 Corinthians 7:28

"But if any man think that he behaveth himself uncomely toward his virgin, if she pass the flower of her age, and need so require, let him do what he will, he sinneth not: let them marry." 1 Corinthians 7:36

"So he that giveth her in marriage doeth well;" 1 Corinthians 7:38

"Marriage is honourable in all, and the bed undefiled: but whoremongers and adulterers God will judge." Hebrews 13:4

The gift of marriage is God given. The desire to find your soul mate and be married is an expression of the gift that is within you.

1. ***God wants those that desire their soul mate to find their soul mate. Mark 11:24***

2. ***God wants those that desire to be married to be married. Hebrews 13:4***

3. ***God wants those that desire to be "joint heirs together of the grace of life" to have that. 1 Peter 3:7b***

4. ***God wants those that have this desire to fulfill this desire so their joy may be full. St. John 16:24***

5. ***God wants you to know that his thoughts toward you are "thoughts of peace (happiness, prosperity, wellness and success), and not of evil (grief, sorrow, trouble and heartaches), to give you an expected end (a future, hope and success). Jeremiah 29:11***

AFFIRMATION THE KEY TO ATTRACTION

Here is a principle so powerful that it seems to be magical and this principle governs the universe and it can create great change for the individual that uses it, it is called Affirmation or Confession.

This principle is a key to bringing about change in your life whether in the form of personal change or bringing new people, things or situations into your life.

Affirmation is speaking forth words out of your mouth of that you want to see happen in your life. Affirmations are an extremely powerful principle, so powerful in fact, that it seems to have the power equivalent to the fairy tale story of

Aladdin's Lamp.

When an individual speaks forth affirmations they are in effect declaring to the God of creation and his universe a statement. Affirmation is another form and definition of the word decree.

The word of God tells us how God used this principle and made a decree concerning things saying: *"When he made a decree for the rain, and a way for the lighting of the thunder: **Then did he see it**, and declare it; he prepared it, yea, and searched it out." Job 28:26-27*

God has also given us this authority to do the same saying; *"Thou shalt also decree a thing, and it shall be established unto thee: and the light shall shine upon thy ways." Job 22:28.* Hallelujah and praise the Lord!

In affirming a thing, it may appear that you're just speaking words into thin air and you're the only one that's hearing the affirmations or confession, but it's just the opposite.

That affirmation and confession that you're speaking forth goes out to God and he responds and causes things to start happening on your behalf. Genesis 1:3-24

The power of confession is only limited by the person's personal conviction and belief that the affirmations are working. The affirmations must not be spoken halfheartedly with doubt, but full of faith that the thing shall come to pass-it shall happen.

If you truly believe what you're affirming then you shall receive the confession of your faith. *"And Jesus answering saith unto them, Have faith in God. For verily I say unto you, That whosoever **shall say** unto this mountain, Be thou* *removed, and be thou cast into the sea; and shall not doubt in his heart,* **but shall believe that those thing he saith** *shall come to pass;* **he shall have whatsoever he saith.***" St. Mark 11:22-23*

You will rise or fall according to that which you're confessing. If you start out with a weak confession and don't sense that faith is in it, stop the confession and go into prayer to get into the presence of God.

When you feel or sense that you've connected in prayer start your affirmation once again out loud and watch faith come. As those words go forth, God responds and brings the manifestation of that which you desire.

Affirmation or confession is the missing revelation in all of life areas. As you begin your confession, let your affirmation be strong and powerful. Be consistent in doing your affirmations. Do them on a daily basis; at night before you go to bed and once again in the morning when you arise and as often during the day as you can.

Speak your affirmations clearly and slowly. Affirm them with feeling and meaning. Don't let lifeless and dull words come out of your mouth, but words full of faith and power, strong and mighty.

Feel the power behind your words. See them as a declaration and proclamation knowing that you are speaking forth that which you desire to see happen in your life.

Don't miss a day of affirming (*if you miss a day, don't get discouraged and give up, but persevere continually*) because you can never retrieve that day.

Daily affirming is vital. It builds up a spirit of consistency that becomes a habit and when something becomes a habit it forms within your character and when your character is formed, it helps creates your destiny.

Destiny is not a matter of chance, but a matter of choice. Your destiny is in your hands. God has done his part and has now commissioned you to do yours by letting your words work for you instead of against you.

AFFIRMATIONS ARE FOR YOUR SUCCESS

As you get started with affirmations, *(I will give you an example of an affirmation for attracting your soul mate)* realize that they are a powerful means for conditioning and renewing your mind so that you can begin to think according to that which you desire. Romans 12:1-2

Next to building up your spirit, nothing is more important than a healthy state of mind, and as your mind is renewed, it in turn affects your spirit and you become strong in both mind and spirit. And then nothing shall be impossible unto you. Mark 11:22-24

GUIDELINES FOR PRACTICING AFFIRMATIONS

Always affirm that something is happening here and now. Do not affirm that something will happen in the future. It's actually a negative confession that says, *"Someday, I will find my soul mate or someday I will be married."* Place the results in today let it be now, *"Now faith is."* Hebrews 11:1

One thing we want to bear hard in this section is that it wont happen overnight. It takes time to build the word into your spirit and renew your mind. It won't happen just because you say it one or two times. Understand it happens as you continually affirm it, it will get into your spirit and become a part of you.

When your affirmations become a part of you then you shall have that which you've confessed and nothing shall be impossible unto you.

AFFIRMATIONS PLUS ACTION EQUALS SUCCESS

As you perform your affirmations on a daily basis there are several ways that God will bring that which you're affirming to pass. In one instance, you may begin to notice that *"hunches"* or *"inspirations"* may come to you to do certain things that will cause that which you've been affirming to come to pass.

Another method God may use is working through other individuals. He may have an individual to tell you something that you need to know that's the answer to what you've been affirming.

He may also use a person to contact you in one manner or another to give you direction about that which you need to know. In most cases the individual being used as an answer may not necessarily know they're the instruments that God is using to bring your affirmation to pass.

Only God and your family members will know about your affirmations for you're doing it in secret, but God will reward you openly. Matthew 6:4. God could use a number of methods to bring your affirmation to pass. He is God and he has all the answers and methods needed to make it happen.

If God uses the method of hunches or inspirations by speaking to your spirit about something to do or say to bring your affirmation into the external world of reality, don't be slothful; put it into action immediately. *Proverbs 12:24. 27,*

15:19, 18:9, 19:15, 24 21:25, 22:13

The thing to remember is that whichever way God chooses you must take action or all your affirming will have been nothing more than a chasing of the wind. You are affirming something that you desire to see happen in your life now-let it happen.

Your affirmation shall come true. It's your job to recognize God's methods and move when he moves, always giving him praise for the answer. When this happens therein lies your destiny and your answer and you shall have that which you desire.

The key word here is action. Make that move act now for *"faith without works (action) is dead." James 2:26.* Now be alert for God's method of manifestation.

THE POWER OF WORDS

"Death and life are in the power of the tongue: and they that love it shall eat the fruit thereof." Proverbs 18:21

Your words are full of power and they will bring forth into your life exactly what comes out of your mouth. Words either create or destroy. They can make your future fruitful or disastrous. You are the architect of your destiny and your words help create your destiny.

Your tongue has within it an awesome source of power, James in his epistle spoke to us concerning the power of the tongue. He understood that man has a powerful instrument in his possession.

Yet, many times man fails to realize the power of his words. Daily he speaks words of negativity, poverty, death, sickness, dissatisfaction, failure etc. Man continually digs a hole for himself deeper and deeper in every area of his life as he daily affirms and confess words of death and destruction.

James said, *"For in many things we offend all.* ***If any man offend not in word,*** *the same is a perfect man, and able also to bridle the whole body. Behold, we put bits in the horses' mouth, that they may obey us; and we turn about their whole body.*

Behold also the ships, which though they be so great, and are driven of fierce winds, yet are they turned about with a very small helm, whithersoever the governor listeth.

Even so the tongue is a little member, and boasteth great things. Behold, how great a matter a little fire kindleth! And the tongue is a fire, a world of iniquity: so is the tongue among our members, that it defileth the whole body, and setteth on fire the course of nature; and it is set on fire of hell.

For every kind of beast, and of birds, and of serpents, and of things in the sea, is tamed, and hath been tamed of mankind: But the tongue can no man tame; it is an unruly evil, full of deadly poison.

Therewith bless we God, even the Father; and therewith curse we men, which are made after the similitude of God. Out of the same mouth proceedeth blessing and cursing. My brethren, these things ought not so to be." James 3:2-10

Your words control your life. Up to this point they have controlled your relationship life and have brought to you just more dates instead of helping you find your soul mate.

From this day forward, your words shall change and you shall begin to speak forth that which you desire to see manifested in your life. It's time for your joy to be made full, for God is faithful that promised. He said *"So shall my word be that goeth forth out of my mouth: it shall not return unto me void, but it shall accomplish that which I please, and it shall prosper in the thing whereto I sent it." Isaiah 55:11*

ATTRACTING YOUR SOUL MATE AFFIRMATIONS

"Even God who quickeneth the dead, and calleth those things which be not as though they were." Romans 4:17

- *Father, I thank you for blessing me to meet my soul mate.*
- *God is now directing the path of my soul mate and I to each other.*
- *A prudent wife is from the Lord and I thank you Father for my wife.*
- *A good godly husband is from the Lord and I thank you Father for my husband.*
- *God has blessed me to find my ideal soul mate and I am so happy.*
- *God's divine intelligence and wisdom knows where this woman/man is and he has ordered our steps toward each other.*
- *My soul mate and I shall recognize each other immediately.*

ATTRACT YOUR IDEAL SOUL MATE BY AFFIRMING

God is now attracting to me my ideal soul mate who is on one accord with me. My soul mate is compatible with me and we blend perfectly together. My soul mate and I love each other and we are the best of friends.

Our relationship is based on the word of God and built upon the solid rock, which is Christ. Because I love this woman/man I can give to her/him the love, happiness and fulfillment she/he needs from the human standpoint.

This woman/man appreciates me for me in spite of my failures and shortcoming and, there is a spiritual and soul connection between us. We are irresistibly attracted to each other and enjoy the company of each other.

We are kind to one another, tenderhearted, forgiving, even as God for Christ's sake hath forgiven us. We walk in love as Christ has loved us and given himself for us.

This woman/man has qualities and attributes that I desire in my soul mate: she/he is spiritual, virtuous, harmonious, faithful, prosperous, honest, loving, a good listener, a good communicator, peaceful, intelligent, wise, passionate and true.

We have confidence in each other and are committed to each other. I thank God for my soul mate and I receive her/him now.

You can also replace anything in this written affirmation that's more to your liking and reword it according to what you desire in your soul mate. You can word it to display qualities and characteristics that you desire in your mate.

Make this affirmation one of the first things you do in the morning and the last thing you do before going to sleep, so that it can get into your spirit, which never sleeps and watch God answer you and bring it to pass.

9
God's Divine Plan
For Your Life

"Call unto me, and I will answer thee, and shew thee great and mighty things, which thou knowest not." Jeremiah 33:3

God has a divine plan for each and every life. Many times in life man has gotten off of God's divine course and allowed people, circumstances and situations to become a part of their lives that were never intended by God.

Many times individuals are dating people that's not God's best choice for their lives and these people have become a part of their lives. Nevertheless, God has given mankind the power to remove any and everything that's not a part of God's divine plan for their lives.

Anything that shouldn't be part of your life should be bound and commanded to go and everything that should be part of your life should be loosed and commanded to come forth for your good. Matthew 16:19

Many times we suffer needlessly when it's within our power to make it good. Affirmations are one of the spiritual weapons that God has given us to use for our good and his glory.

I have personally seen people and things leave my life without saying a word to them about leaving. There were Individuals and things that weren't supposed to be there in the first place. Here is a daily confession for affirming God's divine plan for your life.

God's Divine Plan For Your Life Affirmation

I now bind everything and command every person that's not part of God's divine plan for my life to leave my life now. Matthew 16:19

I now loose everything and call forth the individual(s) that should be part of God's divine plan for my life to come into my life now. God has a divine plan for my life and that divine plan is unfolding for me now. Jeremiah 1:4-5

Nothing can hinder God's divine plan for my life. No one and nothing can delay God's divine plan for my life. What God has for me cannot be diminished. St. John 10:10

The Holy Spirit now reveals, unfolds and manifests God's divine plan for my life quickly, and in peace. Every plan which my heavenly Father has not planned for me is now dissolved. The next step in God's divine plan quickly manifest; God's divine idea, God's divine plan for me now comes to pass. New doors of good now open for me.

10

Meditation Guarantees You Success

"But his delight is in the law of the LORD; and in his law doth he meditate day and night. And he shall be like a tree planted by the rivers of water, that bringeth forth his fruit in his season; his leaf also shall not wither; and whatsoever he doeth shall prosper." Psalm 1:2-3

Throughout the Bible, we see the term meditation over and over again as the key to success in life. In Joshua 1:8 it says, *"This book of the law shall not depart out of thy mouth; but thou shalt meditate therein day and night, that thou mayest observe to do according to all that is written therein: for then thou shalt make thy way prosperous, and then thou shalt have good success."*

Meditation is a lost art in the body of Christ. The devil has made this a most misunderstood topic and has kept the saints away from the use of this powerful spiritual weapon.

When you meditate, you imagine and envision in your mind the outcome of a thing as manifest in your spirit. The Hebrew word for meditate means to actually imagine or see a thing as happening, this is nothing more than faith in action.

If you want to go from just another date to finding your soul mate, you must first come out in the time of meditation through the use of your imagination. See yourself with your ideal soul mate and get a clear mental picture of it just as it shall be when it happens.

Spend time meditating and envisioning you and your soul mate doing the things you would do when you are together in reality.

This may be one of the hardest tasks you will ever have to do, but if you will be consistent with it, you will see the results *"and then thou shalt have good success." Joshua 1:8*

See your soul mate and you spending time together, going out to dinner, going to church, going to the movies and enjoying one another. See all this in as precise detail as you possibly can and have a clear mental picture of this as actually happening.

Hold consistently to your vision with faith and belief; do not waver in the least *"for he that wavereth is like a wave of the sea driven with the wind and tossed. For let not that man think that he shall receive any thing of the Lord. A double minded man is unstable in all his ways." James 1:6-8*

But allow this image and vision to get in your spirit. Do not become discouraged if it seems like you're not progressing; the more you meditate and envision the outcome of you and your soul mate, the more it will get in your spirit and become real.

Having such times of daily envisioning and meditation evokes the thing that you are meditating upon to come forth in your life. As you envision the outcome as manifested in your imagination, you are calling forth by faith, that which you desire. This is faith in action; acting as if your desire is a reality.

1. Faith is calling those things that be not as though they were. Romans 4:17

2. **Faith is moving toward what you hope for just as if you know it shall happen and manifest at the appropriate time.**

3. **Faith is action; it's doing something that draws you toward the manifestation of your beliefs.**

4. **Faith is knowing that God has already set everything in order and we're walking it out in our everyday lives.**

"Now faith is the substance of things hoped for, the evidence of things not seen. For by it the elders obtained a good report. Through faith we understand the worlds were framed by the word of God, so that things which are seen were not made of things which do appear.

Let us draw near with a true heart in full assurance of faith, hold fast the profession of our faith without wavering; (for he is faithful that promises)." Hebrews 11:1-3, 10:22-23

What evidence do we have that faith can do what we desire to see happen, the scriptures tell us saying; *"And what shall I more say? for the time would fail me to tell of Gedeon, and of Barak, and of Samson, and of Jephthae; of David also, and Samuel, and of the prophets:*

Who through faith subdued kingdoms, wrought righteousness, obtained promises, stopped the mouths of lions, Quenched the violence of fire, escaped the edge of the sword, out of weakness were made strong, waxed valiant in fight, turned to flight the armies of the aliens. Women received their dead raised to life again." Hebrews 11:32-35

If God can do all these things through faith, surely he can orchestrate the destiny of you and your soul mate bringing you both together by his divine understanding and wisdom.

Meditation guarantees your success. While Isaac was waiting for Abraham's servant to return with the lady that would be his soul mate and wife, the scriptures say: *"And Isaac went out to meditate in the field at the eventide: and he lifted up his eyes, and saw, and, behold, the camels were coming.*

And Rebekah lifted up her eyes, and when she saw Isaac, she lighted off the camel. For she had said unto the servant, What man is this that walketh in the field to meet us? And the servant had said, It is my master: therefore she took a vail, and covered herself.

And the servant told Isaac all things that he had done. And Isaac brought her into his mother Sarah's tent, and took Rebekah, and she became his wife; and he loved her: and Isaac was comforted after his mother's death." Genesis 24:63-67

Once again, Meditation in action bringing forth success and it always manifests in the external realm of reality.

Your Soul Mate Desire Chart

A soul mate desire chart is a chart that displays your 10 desires that you want in your soul mate. A soul mate chart is like producing a profile of the person that you desire to find or be found by. Your soul mate chart helps to clarify the type of soul mate you desire so that you will know exactly what you're seeking. Once you get a clear mental image of your soul mate this enables you to present with clarity your desire to God and puts out a blueprint of your desire throughout the earth.

Your soul mate desire chart is your detailed outline of your specific soul mate choice. It is your plan of action for finding or being found of your soul mate. It is the essential features or main aspects that you believe will enable you to have a successful and blessed relationship and marriage.

One note that I would like to make is to be always open to God who knows all things from the beginning to the end. Your chart gives God and you something to work with and focus on to create faith in your heart. If one or two out of the ten things does not totally line up but eight or nine things does and you have a witness and peace in your spirit don't try to hold out for all ten.

Realize that ultimately God is the only one that knows what you really need and these eight or nine things that he/she possess will be the essential and vital qualities that you will need in your soul mate to enjoy the celebration of love that you need to make it a success. The scripture says, *" A man's heart deviseth his ways: but the LORD directeth his steps." Proverbs 16:9*

SOUL MATE DESIRE CHART

"Here are my 10 desires that my soul mate possess."

1. Spiritual =

2. Physical =

3. Financial =

4. Mental =

5. Social =

6. Secular =

7. Ministry =

8. Marital =

9. Activities =

10. Values =

You can either write them out here or you can take a sheet of paper and write them out. Take out time to meditate on this chart, you can do 30 minutes of daily imagining this person in your life. You can either do two 15 minute sessions or three 10 minute session, which ever is more convient for you. In your meditation time you will see yourself with this person, you will imagine this person and you enjoying life together in every way. Now, take this time to write out your soul mate chart for your soul mate awaits.

11

God's Ideal Relationship

"The voice of my beloved! Behold, he cometh leaping upon the mountains, skipping upon the hills. My beloved is like a roe or a young hart: behold, he standeth behind our wall, he looketh forth at the windows, shewing himself through the lattice. My beloved spake, and said unto me, Rise up, my love, my fair one, and come away." Song of Solomon 2:8-10

The closest idea we have of a harmonious and compatible relationship of two people in love is exemplified in the scriptures according to the Song of Solomon. Here we have two people that are obviously soul mates.

The communication and attraction between these two people displays love of the highest order; it shows respect, consideration, passion, compassion, kindness, unselfishness, patience, temperance, faith, hope and belief.

Notice, the terminology which they use and the easy display of verbal affection to one another, the honesty, sincerity and excitement of just being in one another's presence. We don't attempt to interpret the words of these two individuals that are wonderfully in love. We just give it to you as it is and allow the Holy Spirit to enlighten your mind and speak to your spirit as you read it.

Notice the love and beauty of it all as we listen to two people that are immensely in love with one another as it should be. Listen as the emotions run high and the feelings of each are spoken effortlessly. There is no holding back here because each desire the other to know what they think and how they feel. Read it slowly and observe the words they're speaking.

Let us now behold *"The song of songs, which is Solomon's. Let him kiss me with the kisses of his mouth: for thy love is better than wine. Because of the savour of thy good ointments thy name is as ointment poured forth, therefore do the virgins love thee.*

Draw me, we will run after thee: the king hath brought me into his chambers: we will be glad and rejoice in thee, we will remember thy love more than wine: the upright love thee.

I am black, but comely, O ye daughters of Jerusalem, as the tents of Kedar, as the curtains of Solomon. Look not upon me, because I am black, because the sun hath looked upon me: my mother's children were angry with me; they made me the keeper of the vineyards; but mine own vineyard have I not kept.

Tell me, O thou whom my soul loveth, where thou feedest, where thou makest thy flock to rest at noon: for why should I be as one that turneth aside by the flocks of thy companions?

If thou know not, O thou fairest among women, go thy way forth by the footsteps of the flock, and feed thy kids beside the shepherds' tents. I have compared thee, O my love, to a company of horses in Pharaoh's chariots.

Thy cheeks are comely with rows of jewels, thy neck with chains of gold. We will make thee borders of gold with studs of silver. While the king sitteth at his table, my spikenard sendeth forth the smell thereof.

A bundle of myrrh is my well-beloved unto me; he shall lie all night betwixt my breasts. My beloved is unto me as a cluster of camphire in the vineyards of En-gedi. Behold, thou art fair, my love; behold, thou art fair; thou hast doves' eyes. Behold, thou art fair, my beloved, yea, pleasant: also our bed is green. The beams of our house are cedar, and our rafters of fir.

I am the rose of Sharon, and the lily of the valleys. As the lily among thorns, so is my love among the daughters. As the apple tree among the trees of the wood, so is my beloved among the sons. I sat down under his shadow with great delight, and his fruit was sweet to my taste. He brought me to the banqueting house, and his banner over me was love.

Stay me with flagons, comfort me with apples: for I am sick of love. His left hand is under my head, and his right hand doth embrace me. I charge you, O ye daughters of Jerusalem, by the roes, and by the hinds of the field, that ye stir not up, nor awake my love, till he please.

The voice of my beloved! behold, he cometh leaping upon the mountains, skipping upon the hills. My beloved is like a roe or a young hart: behold, he standeth behind our wall, he looketh forth at the windows, shewing himself through the lattice.

My beloved spake, and said unto me, Rise up, my love, my fair one, and come away. For, lo, the winter is past, the rain is over and gone; The flowers appear on the earth; the time of the singing of birds is come, and the voice of the turtle is heard in our land; The fig tree putteth forth her green figs, and the vines with the tender grape give a good smell.

Arise, my love, my fair one, and come away. O my dove, that art in the clefts of the rock, in the secret places of the stairs, let me see thy countenance, let me hear thy voice; for sweet is thy voice, and thy countenance is comely.

Take us the foxes, the little foxes, that spoil the vines: for our vines have tender grapes. My beloved is mine, and I am his: he feedth among the lilies. Until the day break, and the shadows flee away, turn, my beloved, and be thou like a roe or a young hart upon the mountains of Bether.

By night on my bed I sought him whom my soul loveth: I sought him, but I found him not. I will rise now, and go about the city in the streets, and in the broad ways I will seek him whom my soul loveth: I sought him, but I found him not.

The watchmen that go about the city found me: to whom I said, Saw ye him whom my soul loveth? It was but a little that I passed from them, but I found him whom my soul loveth: I held him, and would not let him go, until I had brought him into my mother's house, and into the chamber of her that conceived me.

I charge you, O ye daughters of Jerusalem, by the roes, and by the hinds of the field, that ye stir not up, nor awake my love, till he please. Who is this that cometh out of the wilderness like pillars of smoke, perfumed with myrrh and frankincense, with all powders of the merchant?

Behold his bed, which is Solomon's; threescore valiant men are about it, of the valiant of Israel. They all hold swords, being expert in war: every man hath his sword upon his thigh because of fear in the night.

King Solomon made himself a chariot of the wood of Lebanon. He made pillars thereof of silver, the bottom thereof of gold, the covering of it of purple, the midst thereof being paved with love, for the daughters of Jerusalem.

Go forth, O ye daughters of Zion, and behold king Solomon with the crown wherewith his mother crowned him in the day of his espousals, and in the day of the gladness of his heart.

Behold, thou art fair, my love; behold, thou art fair; thou hast doves' eyes within thy locks: thy hair is as a flock of goats, that appear from mount Gilead. Thy teeth are like a flock of sheep that are even shorn, which came up from the washing; whereof every one bear twins, and none is barren among them.

Thy lips are like a thread of scarlet, and thy speech is comely: thy temples are like a piece of a pomegranate within thy locks. Thy neck is like the tower of David builded for an armoury, whereon there hang a thousand bucklers, all shields of mighty men.

Thy two breasts are like two young roes that are twins, which feed among the lilies. Until the day break, and the shadows flee away, I will get me to the mountain of myrrh, and to the hill of frankincense.

Thou art all fair, my love; there is no spot in thee. Come with me from Lebanon, my spouse, with me from Lebanon: look from the top of Amana, from the top of Shenir and Hermon, from the lions' dens, from the mountains of the leopards.

Thou hast ravished my heart, my sister, my spouse; thou hast ravished my heart with one of thine eyes, with one chain of thy neck. How fair is thy love, my sister, my spouse! how much better is thy love than wine! and the smell of thine ointments than all spices!

Thy lips, O my spouse, drop as the honeycomb: honey and milk are under thy tongue; and the smell of thy garments is like the smell of Lebanon. A garden inclosed is my sister, my spouse; a spring shut up, a fountain sealed.

Thy plants are an orchard of pomegranates, with pleasant fruits; camphire, with spikenard, Spikenard and saffron; calamus and cinnamon, with all trees of frankincense; myrrh and aloes, with all the chief spices: A fountain of gardens, a well of living waters, and streams from Lebanon.

Awake, O north wind; and come, thou south; blow upon my garden, that the spices thereof may flow out. Let my beloved come into his garden and eat his pleasant fruits.

I am come into my garden, my sister, my spouse: I have gathered my myrrh with my spice; I have eaten my honeycomb with my honey; I have drunk my wine with my milk: eat, O friends; drink, yea, drink abundantly, O beloved.

I sleep, but my heart waketh: it is the voice of my beloved that knocketh, saying, Open to me, my sister, my love, my dove, my undefiled: for my head is filled with dew, and my locks with the drops of the night.

I have put off my coat; how shall I put it on? I have washed my feet; how shall I defile them? My beloved put in his hand by the hole of the door, and my bowels were moved for him.

I rose up to open to my beloved; and my hand dropped with myrrh, and my fingers with sweet smelling myrrh, upon the handles of the lock. I opened to my beloved; but my beloved had withdrawn himself, and was gone: my soul failed when he spake: I sought him, but I could not find him; I called him, but he gave me no answer.

The watchmen that went about the city found me, they smote me, they wounded me; the keepers of the walls took away my veil from me. I charge you, O daughter of Jerusalem, if ye find my beloved, that ye tell him, that I am sick of love.

What is thy beloved more than another beloved, O thou fairest among women? what is thy beloved more than another beloved, that thou dost so charge us?

My beloved is white and ruddy, the chiefest among ten thousand. His head is as the most fine gold, his locks are bushy, and black as a raven. His eyes are as the eyes of doves by the rivers of water, washed with milk, and fitly set.

His cheeks are as a bed of spices, as sweet flowers: his lips like lilies, dropping sweet smelling myrrh. His hands are as gold rings set with the beryl: his belly is as bright ivory overlaid with sapphires.

His legs are as pillars of marble, set upon sockets of fine gold: his countenance is as Lebanon, excellent as the cedars. His mouth is most sweet: yea, he is altogether lovely. **This is my beloved, and this is my friend,** *O daughters of Jerusalem.*

Whither is thy beloved gone, O thou fairest among women? whither is thy beloved turned aside? that we may seek him with thee. My beloved is gone down into his garden, to the bed of spices, to feed in the gardens, and to gather lilies.

I am my beloved's, and my beloved is mine: he feedeth among the lilies. Thou art beautiful, O my love, as Tirzah, comely as Jerusalem, terrible as an army with banners. Turn away thine eyes from me, for they have overcome me: thy hair is as a flock of goats that appear from Gilead.

Thy teeth are as a flock of sheep which go up from the washing, whereof every one beareth twins, and there is not one barren among them. As a piece of a pomegranate are thy temples within thy locks. There are threescore queens, and fourscore concubines, and virgins without number.

My dove, my undefiled is but one; she is the only one of her mother, she is the choice one of her that bare her. The daughters saw her, and blessed her; yea, the queens and the concubines, and they praised her.

Who is she that looketh forth as the morning, fair as the moon, clear as the sun, and terrible as an army with banners? I went down into the garden of nuts to see the fruits of the valley, and to see whether the vine flourished, and the pomegranates budded.

Or ever I was aware, my soul made me like the chariots of Ammi-nadib. Return, return, O Shulamite; return, return, that we may look upon thee. What will ye see in the Shulamite? As it were the company of two armies.

How beautiful are thy feet with shoes, O prince's daughter! the joints of thy thighs are like jewels, the work of the hands of a cunning workman. Thy navel is like a round goblet, which wanteth not liquor: thy belly is like an heap of wheat set about with lilies.

Thy two breasts are like two young roes that are twins. Thy neck is as a tower of ivory: thine eyes like the fishpools in Heshbon, by the gate of Bath-rabbim: thy nose is as the tower of Lebanon which looketh toward Damascus.

Thine head upon thee is like Carmel, and the hair of thine head like purple; the king is held in the galleries. How fair and how pleasant art thou, O love, for delights! This thy stature is like to a palm tree, and thy breasts to clusters of grapes.

I said, I will go up to the palm tree, I will take hold of the boughs thereof: now also thy breasts shall be as the clusters of the vine, and the smell of thy nose like apples; And the roof of thy mouth like the best wine for my beloved, that goeth down sweetly, causing the lips of those that are asleep to speak.

I am my beloved's, and his desire is toward me. Come, my beloved, let us go forth into the field; let us lodge in the villages. Let us get up early to the vineyards; let us see if the vine flourish, whether the tender grape appear, and the pomegranates bud forth: there will I give thee my love.

The mandrakes give a smell, and at our gates are all manner of pleasant fruits, new and old, which I have laid up for thee, O my beloved.

O that thou wert as my brother, that sucked the breasts of my mother! when I should find thee without, I would kiss thee; yea, I should not be despised. I would lead thee, and bring thee into my mother's house, who would instruct me: I would cause thee to drink of spiced wine of the juice of my pomegranate.

His left hand should be under my head, and his right hand should embrace me. I charge you, O daughters of Jerusalem, that ye stir not up, nor awake my love, until he pleased.

Who is this that cometh up from the wilderness, leaning upon her beloved? I raised thee up under the apple tree: there thy mother brought thee forth: there she brought thee forth that bare thee.

Set me as a seal upon thine heart, as a seal upon thine arm: for love is strong as death; jealousy is cruel as the grave: the coals thereof are coals of fire, which hath a most vehement flame.

Many waters cannot quench love, neither can the floods drown it: if a man would give all the substance of his house for love, it would be utterly contemned. We have a little sister, and she hath no breasts: what shall we do for our sister in the day when she shall be spoken for?

If she be a wall, we will build upon her a palace of silver: and if she be a door, we will inclose her with boards of cedar. I am a wall, and my breasts like towers; then was I in his eyes as one that found favour.

Solomon had a vineyard at Baal-hamon; he let out the vineyard unto keepers; everyone for the fruit thereof was to bring a thousand pieces of silver. My vineyard, which is mine, is before me: thou, O Solomon, must have a thousand, and those that keep the fruit thereof two hundred.

Thou that dwellest in the gardens, the companions hearken to thy voice: cause me to hear it. Make hast, my beloved, and be thou like to a roe or to a young hart upon the mountain of spices." Song of Solomon 1-8

12

The Ten Elements of Truth

"Every way of a man is right in his own eyes: but he LORD pondereth the hearts." Proverbs 21:2

In this section, we will list 10 elements of truth for a successful relationship and marriage and we will also list 10 elements of truth that will cause failure and sorrow in a relationship and marriage.

10 ELEMENTS OF TRUTH FOR SUCCESS

1. Because you're in love with each other.
2. Because you've found your ideal soul mate.
3. Because you're highly compatible with each other.
4. Because you're both following the word of God faithfully.
5. Because you have a witness and peace in your spirit.
6. Because you're intimate with each other (not sexual) but best friends.
7. Because there is a spiritual and soul connection between the two of you.
8. Because there is a physical attraction between the two of you.
9. Because you love and appreciate each other in spite of the failures and shortcomings of the other.
10. Because you have confidence in each other and have made a commitment to each other.

10 ELEMENTS OF TRUTH FOR FAILURE

1. Because your clock is ticking.
2. Because you want to have sex and intimacy only.

3. Because you've gotten pregnant.
4. Because you are being pressured by your parents, relatives, friends etc.
5. Because you want financial gain and prosperity.
6. Because you want to lift your ego or have social status.
7. Because you want someone to take care of you.
8. Because you're feeling lonely.
9. Because you want someone to be a father or mother to your children.
10. Because there is a physical attraction alone.

Follow the 10 elements of truth for a successful relationship and marriage and happiness and intimacy with your soul mate and spouse will be within your reach.

Follow the 10 elements of truth for failure in a relationship and marriage and you will experience a broken heart and a lifetime of sorrow.

13

Ten Ways To Know If You Have Met Your Soul Mate

Wouldn't it be nice to know right away if the person that you're talking with is the individual that is to be your soul mate and life mate? Well, you can know by simply knowing what to look for and by knowing yourself. Here are the 10 ways to know if you have met your soul mate.

1. Know yourself and know what type of characteristics, traits and personality you want in a soul mate and don't deviate and accept less than what you know you are satisfied with. DOES THAT PERSON MATCH THAT?

2. Do you have a witness and peace in your spirit and heart about this individual in your life? If you do not then slow it down and make sure that you are led of the Spirit.

3. The two of you seem to naturally flow together; there is a great spiritual and soul (mental) connection between the two of you.

4. To look at this person is like looking at an image of yourself.

5. When you've met your soul mate the two of you will display the utmost honesty and support for one another and this person will make you (the female) feel beautiful and satisfied. This person will make you (the male) feel like you're very worthy and able to accomplish anything.

6. With your soul mate it's like you've known this person for a long time even though the time has been brief.

7. Your soul mate and you are very harmonious and can work well together.

8. The both of you are very supportive of one another and desire to see growth in each other in every area of life.

9. Your soul mate accepts you for you; they're not in the business of trying to change you. They're like a best friend.

10. Your soul mate adores the time they have with you and aren't afraid to make a commitment to you.

- There is no such thing as 100% agreement on all things; however, the ideal soul mate for you is one where the two of you will blend perfectly together.

- Your ideal soul mate is one where the two of you have a shared purpose in life with the capacity to enable each other to develop and grow spiritually, emotionally and mentally.

- It doesn't mean that the person is perfect and without flaw, but he or she is perfect for you. However, as stated earlier that same person may be a disastrous relationship with someone else. This doesn't mean that the person is bad, only that they're not the best choice for someone else.

- It's okay to understand that everyone will not blend with you no matter how good you may see yourself, it's not a reflection on you, it's just a red light that this is not a go between the two of you.

- **If a person is not attracted to you don't try to force it and make an attraction. You cannot make someone attracted to you that feel no chemistry between the two of you.**

Also, you will notice that we have said nothing about finances. Even though finances are of vital importance, it's not going to make you have a truly happy and successful relationship and marriage.

Finances, though very important cannot reach the heart and minister to the soul and spirit of the individual; it's a by-product that's needed to help make a prosperous and materially blessed relationship and marriage.

Plus, when you meet your soul mate the two of you can go forth and make all the money you need because you have found each other. As a team and partners nothing will be impossible for the two of you to accomplish.

There are many financially prosperous relationships and marriages at this very moment that are empty and void of life, passion, love, romance, compassion, communication etc.

Many relationships would trade all their finances for a moment of true love, romance, compassion and communication, for this is their true heart cry and longing. This is something that only your true soul mate can fulfill and supply in abundance and without reservation for they are the one that is destined to satisfy that place which God has left in your heart for them to fill.

Notice also, we did not put great emphasis on looks or physical attraction, even though this is of great importance this should not be priority number one on your list. Physical attraction will eventually fade; it's the heart (spirit) and mind of the individual that should be first and foremost in your mind, afterwards physical attraction.

There are many individuals with some of the most beautiful ladies and the most handsome men, but there is no true love, passion, romance, compassion communication etc, in their relationship or marriage.

Many times it mostly a sexual thing, but deep down its dead and void of life and the ***physical attraction alone*** cannot produce the celebration of love that a true relationship and marriage needs to last.

Follow these instructions and you will know whether you have met your soul mate or just another date.

14

Ten Questions to Ask to Determine Whether Or Not You've Met Your Soul Mate

In the dating game I've always wished there were a set of questions that I could ask so that I would know right away whether I was talking with an individual that has the possibility of being a true potential soul mate or just another date.

Well now you can know, here are 10 questions to ask to see if you've met your soul mate or just another date. Here are the 10 questions you've always wanted to know but didn't know whom to ask. They are a must for anyone ready to date, dating or engaged.

1. *Tell me 2 things about yourself, how others would describe you and 2 bad habits.*

2. *Tell me what is your one great heart desire.*

3. *What are your spiritual beliefs about God and the Bible and what types of music do you like?*

4. *What are your goals in life and tell me 3 things that you like to do that bring you great satisfaction?*

5. *How would you describe your past relationships, what did you learn and what would you do differently?*

6. *What type of relationship are you looking for and what does romance mean to you and how important*

is sex in marriage?

7. *What would you say are 3 important things for a successful relationship?*

8. *How could you enhance my life and in what way(s) would you be an asset to me?*

9. *How important is spending time in God's word, prayer and church attendance to you?*

10. *How important is spending time doing things together to you and what are your thoughts about kids?*

These 10 questions are designed to let you know what is in the heart or spirit of the individual so that you can make an intelligent decision about whether to continue getting to know this individual giving out your time, energy and money in this association.

The way to get to know an individual is by getting them to talk; communication is the key. The scriptures say, *"For out of the abundance of the heart the mouth speaketh."* (Matthew 12:34b)

These 10 questions will give you an insight into the life, personality, goals and characteristics of the individual you're talking with and will allow you to rate those questions by scoring each question in sequence.

Do not accept one-word answers have the individual to go into some depth with each question.

You can rate these questions by giving each a score of 0 to 3, here is how each number will rate the individual.

- *0 is considered Disastrous.*
- *1 is considered Poor.*
- *2 is considered Average.*
- *3 is considered Excellent.*

If the individual you're giving the questions to score less than 25 at the conclusion of the questions you need to forget about this from a relationship standpoint and let this be just a friendship or association type relationship.

No need to waste anymore time, money or energy with this from a soul mate and life mate perspective.

If the individual scores 25 or more you have a high probability for a successful, harmonious and long lasting relationship.

There are no right or wrong answers or scores but in order for you to have a successful relationship with the right individual there must be a score of 25 or more.

- *A low score is 21.*
- *Most individuals will continue in a relationship with scores of 19, 20, and 21, but they don't last and fails to be productive and fulfilling.*
- *Successful relationships scores between the 25 and 30 range.*

For example, suppose you meet someone and you give him or her the test and they score 22. Remember, they should score at least 25 before you can get excited about them. The scoring gives you an opportunity to see where you'll lack in this relationship and in marriage if you choose to pursue it anyway.

HERE ARE FIVE GUIDELINES TO FOLLOW WHEN USING THIS SYSTEM!

1. Don't put a lot of time, energy and money into an association until you have had the opportunity to give the individual your questions. If you're already in a relationship give them the questions anyway so that you can know whether you are with your soul mate or just another date.

2. Using these questions can save yourself a broken heart and broken promises. Remember, if they fail these questions you're going to have to choose whether to continue in that relationship or break it off, make it easy on yourself and do it right the first time.

3. If these questions seems like you're probing it's better to know these things up front now than have to find out the truth later and wished you had asked these simple questions in the beginning.

4. If an individual gets upset about these questions take notice at this, for they either have something to hide or they're just not the one that's right for you (*remember, your soul mate is not afraid of commitment and honesty*), they're definitely not your soul mate. These questions can save you a lifetime of troubles.

5. If you've already fallen in love with the individual and they fail the questions you will have to decide whether you want to continue with this relationship

and settle for less than the best for your life. If you decide to continue then you will have to deal with the consequences and settle for a life with just another date and not your true soul mate.

If you don't want to give the individual the questions on paper, you can learn the questions yourself and ask them throughout a conversation or several conversations. These questions are designed to inform you who this individual is and what you will be in store for. Are you willing to settle for Just Another Date for the rest of your life? Or do you want to spend the rest of your life with your ideal Soul Mate? These questions will enable you to know upfront so that you can make the best choice possible.

15

Twelve Authoritative Prayers To Bind And Blast Away Just Another Date

"And whatsoever you shall bind on earth shall be bound in heaven." Matthew 16:19

Here are 12 Authoritative prayers that you can use to bind and blast away just more dates. From this day forward begin to take authority over your relationship life and determine your destiny by orchestrating it in prayer.

At this point go to God in prayer and confess any known sin to the Lord and repent of anything that may stand between you and God. Ask him to forgive you and cleanse you by his precious blood.

Next, take about 5 minutes and begin to spend time in praises to the Lord, thanking him for who he is and what he has done for you and what he shall do for you in bringing you your soul mate.

Now, enter into this time of prayer with aggressive and bold praying. Pray these prayers repeatedly with determination and faith until you see the manifestation of your desire.

1. I bind just more dates from coming into my life from this day forward in Jesus name.

2. I refuse to waste my time with individuals that aren't sent by God to be in my life in the name of Jesus.

3. No weapon that is formed against me shall prosper in the name of Jesus.

4. I reject unrighteous associations that try to become a part of my life in Jesus name.

5. I release myself from the spirit of divorces and unstable relationships in the name of Jesus.

6. Every spirit of instability in relationships I detach myself from you in the name of Jesus.

7. I break the spirit of familiarity that has caused me to attach myself to people that have been wrong for me in the past in the name of Jesus.

8. Every satanic influence that has led me astray in relationships the hand of God is against you in Jesus name.

9. Every satanic deception; the fire of God is against you in Jesus name.

10. Every seducing spirit; the Lord rebukes you in Jesus name.

11. Every hidden agenda come to light and be bound in Jesus name.

12. I reject all that are transformed as an angle of light, but are sent by Satan to destroy and prevent my marital destiny in Jesus name.

16

Twelve Authoritative Prayers To Loose And Attract Your Soul Mate

"And whatsoever ye shall loose on earth shall be loosed in heaven." Matthew 16:19

Here are 12 Authoritative Prayers you can use to Loose and Attract Your Soul Mate. Pray these prayers in the same manner which you prayed the prayers above and watch God attract to you your soul mate and life mate.

1. I loose the Spirit of God to attract to me the individual that God has destined to be my soul mate and life mate in the name of Jesus.

2. Father, I commit my life to you and thank you for directing me toward the individual that is my soul mate in Jesus name.

3. Father, I give you praise that I'm hidden under your shadow so that only my soul mate can find me in Jesus name.

4. The blood of Jesus protects me from every encounter that's not the destiny of my soul mate and I in the name of Jesus.

5. My relationship life lives now by the resurrection power of the Lord Jesus Christ.

6. The Holy Spirit of God leads me into all truth in relationships in Jesus name.

7. The angel of the Lord encamps about me and delivers me from every satanic plan in the name of Jesus.

8. Father, I thank you for stretching forth your mighty hand to perform signs and wonders in my relationship life in Jesus name.

9. My prayer now attracts to me the soul mate that God has destined for my life in the name of Jesus.

10. The anointing of God destroys every yoke that comes against me in Jesus name.

11. Father, I thank you for your divine intervention on my behalf in the name of Jesus.

12. Lord, thank you for releasing the spirit of attraction that attracts to me my ideal soul mate in the name of Jesus.

17

Walk in Love

"I therefore, the prisoner of the Lord, beseech you that that ye walk worthy of the vocation wherewith ye are called. With all lowliness and meekness, with longsuffering, forbearing one another in love; Endeavoring to keep the unity of the Spirit in the bond of peace." Ephesians 4:1-3

What better way to end this book than a chapter that speaks on walking in love for love is the fulfilling of every law. As people of God we should be loving people and exemplify the love of God in our lives, for the scripture says; *"because the love of God is shed abroad in our hearts by the Holy Ghost which is given unto us." Romans 5:5*

Take the love test and see if you're walking in love according to the scriptures and if not *"let love be"* for love is in you desiring to come out of you and be shed abroad upon others.

Love is the greatest of all and no matter what else you may have or do, without love you're building a foundation upon sand. Jesus said *"And every one that heareth these sayings of mine, and doeth them not, shall be likened unto a foolish man, which built his house upon the sand: And the rain descended, and the floods came, and the winds blew, and beat upon that house; and it fell: and great was the fall of it." Matthew 7:26-27*

THE GREATEST OF THESE IS LOVE

"Though I speak with the tongues of men and of angels, and have not charity (love), I am become as sounding brass, or a tinkling cymbal. And though I have the gift of prophecy, and understand all mysteries, and all knowledge; and though I have all faith, so that I could remove mountains, and have not charity (love), I am nothing.

And though I bestow all my goods to feed the poor, and though I give my body to be burned, and have not charity (love), it profiteth me nothing.

Charity suffereth long, and is kind; charity envieth not; charity vaunteth not itself, is not puffed up, Doth not behave itself unseemly, seeketh not her own, is not easily provoked, thinketh no evil;

Rejoiceth not in iniquity, but rejoiceth in the truth; Beareth all things, believeth all things, hopeth all things, endureth all things.

Charity never faileth: but whether there be prophecies, they shall fail; whether there be tongues, they shall cease; whether there be knowledge, it shall vanish away.

For we know in part, and we prophesy in part. But when that which is perfect is come, then that which is in part shall be done away. When I was a child, I spake as a child, I understood as a child, I thought as a child: but when I became a man, I put away childish things.

For now we see through a glass, darkly' but then face to face: now I know in part; but then shall I know even as also I am known. And now abideth faith, hope, charity, these three; but the greatest of these is charity." 1 Corinthians 13

The Greatest Relationship of All

As God's servants we could not with all good conscience end this book without offering you the opportunity to experience the greatest relationship of all. All other relationships pale in comparison to establishing a relationship with your creator and maker. *"For he hath made him to be sin for us, who knew no sin; that we might be made the righteousness of God in him. He that spared not his own Son, but delivered him up for us all, how shall he not with him also freely give us all things?" 2 Corinthians 5:21, Romans 8:32*

God wants a relationship with you and he gave his Son who gave his life for you and me to reconcile us to God. *"For when we were yet without strength, in due time Christ died for the ungodly. For scarcely for a righteous man will one die: yet peradventure for a good man some would even dare to die. But God commendeth his love toward us, in that, while we were yet sinners, Christ died for us." Romans 5:6-8*

You can receive Jesus Christ into your life right now as your Lord and Savior and receive eternal life. It's simple really, you just ask Jesus to come into your life with this simple prayer:

"Dear God, according to your word I have sinned and come short of the glory of God. I stand in need of the Savior Jesus Christ. I repent of my sins and ask Jesus to come into my life. I acknowledge that I am a sinner and need to be saved. I believe that Jesus died, was resurrected and is now alive at your right hand. I ask that the blood of Jesus cleanse me from all sins and I accept Jesus into my life now. Father, I thank you for receiving me, I am now a child of God, I'm saved and my name is written in the lambs book of life, in Jesus name. Amen"

Tell us about your decision in receiving Jesus Christ as your Lord and Savior, we will get you out some literature as soon as possible, God bless you and keep you.

You can also email us at soulmateorjustadate@yahoo.com or visit our web site at www.abundantliferevivalcenter.org or www.deliverancepower.org

Printed in the United States
203907BV00002B/370-471/P